THE AUSTRALIAN
Women's Weekly
more
kids' cakes

acp
books

contents

The oven temperatures in this book are for
conventional ovens; if you have a fan-forced oven,
decrease the temperature by 10-20 degrees.

perfectly pretty

fairy trellis

equipment

deep 15cm (6-inch) round cake pan
20cm (8-inch) round prepared cake
   board (page 110) or cake stand
3 small piping bags
1 large piping bag fitted with
   small plain tube

cake

470g (15-ounce) packaged
   buttercake mix
1 quantity fluffy frosting (page 107)
green, pink and yellow food colouring

decorations

375g (12 ounces) white chocolate melts
piped sugar roses
fairy ornament
ribbon

1 Preheat oven to 150°C/300°F. Grease cake pan; line base and side with baking paper, extending paper 5cm (2 inches) above side.
2 Make cake according to directions on packet. Pour enough mixture into pan to fill to three-quarters (use any leftover mixture to make cupcakes for another occasion). Bake cake about 1 hour. Stand cake in pan 5 minutes; turn cake, top-side up, onto wire rack to cool.
3 Meanwhile, squash and press a large piece of foil into a cylindrical shape, with a base of 8cm (3 inches) and a height of 15cm (6 inches). Round the top of the cylinder. Stand the foil shape in a glass or cup to make it stable.
4 Stir chocolate in medium heatproof bowl over medium saucepan of simmering water until melted (do not allow water to touch bottom of bowl). Tint about 1 tablespoon melted chocolate pink, another tablespoon yellow and another tablespoon green.

Place each colour into separate small paper piping bags (page 114); pipe different-sized discs of chocolate onto baking-paper-lined tray. Tap tray on bench to make discs level; stand at room temperature until set.
5 Tint remaining melted chocolate green for trellis; pour into large piping bag. Using pattern from pattern sheet, pipe chocolate over trellis pattern, starting with rectangle and inside lines first.
6 Just before chocolate sets, drape chocolate rectangle over foil cylinder to shape trellis; set at room temperature.
7 Level top of cake, position cake, cut-side down, on cake board; secure cake with a little frosting. Tint fluffy frosting green; spread all over cake. Gently peel baking paper from trellis, position trellis on cake before frosting sets.
8 Use tiny dabs of leftover frosting to attach roses to trellis. Position chocolate discs and fairy in garden.
9 When frosting has set, wind ribbon through trellis.

Shaped foil cylinder

Piping trellis

Shaping trellis

tips Pipe chocolate for
the trellis quite thickly to
make it strong. If the trellis
breaks, re-melt the chocolate
and make the trellis again.
The chocolate should be
almost set before shaping
the trellis. This cake can be
made a day before the party.

tips Mark the quilting on the bag before the icing becomes firm. Dots can be positioned on the cake before or after the icing has set. Be sure to remove the the toothpicks before cake is served. This cake can be made two days ahead; position the handle just before the party.

quilted handbag

two 14cm x 21cm (5½-inch x 8½-inch)
   loaf pans
20cm x 30cm (8-inch x 12-inch)
   rectangular prepared cake board
    (page 110) or cake stand
plastic ruler
3 strong wooden toothpicks
fine artist's paint brush

cake

3 x 470g (15-ounce) packaged
   buttercake mix
1kg (2 pounds) ready-made
   white icing (page 107)
1 cup (160g) pure icing
   (confectioners') sugar
purple food colouring
1 cup (320g) apricot jam (conserve),
   warmed, strained

decorations

1 yellow conversation heart
1 marshmallow rope

1 Preheat oven to 150°C/300°F. Grease and flour loaf pans.
2 Make cakes according to directions on packet. Divide mixture evenly between pans; bake about 1¼ hours. Turn cakes, top-side up, onto wire rack to cool.
3 Knead ready-made icing on surface dusted with sifted icing sugar until icing loses its stickiness; tint mauve.
4 Trim tops of cakes to make them as flat as possible and the same depth.
5 Join cut sides of cakes with some of the jam to form the handbag. Trim the bottom of the handbag to make it sit flat. Stand cake, on its trimmed long side, on cake board. Brush cake all over with more jam.
6 Roll three-quarters of the icing on sugared surface until large enough to cover cake. Using rolling pin, lift icing onto cake, smooth icing over cake with sugared hands. Trim icing neatly around base of cake (page 112).

7 Starting from the centre of the back of cake, use side of ruler to gently mark icing into diagonal shapes before icing sets (page 88).
8 Roll out remaining icing on sugared surface. Using paper pattern from pattern sheet, cut out flap for handbag. Position flap on cake. Dab a tiny amount of jam on the front of the heart lolly, position on bag for clasp. Push one toothpick under the heart through the cake to support the clasp.
9 Using sugared hands, roll tiny balls of soft icing from the scraps. Using the end of the paint brush, make tiny indents in the icing, where the quilting lines cross; dab a tiny amount of water into each indent, gently push a ball of icing into each indent.
10 Cut marshmallow rope to length required for handle of bag, push a toothpick into each end of the rope, leaving about 1cm (½ inch) of toothpick exposed to push into the cake.
11 Position handle just before serving.

daisy chain

equipment

deep 20cm (8-inch) square cake pan
25cm (10-inch) square prepared
    cake board (page 110)
small piping bag fitted with
    small plain tube

cake

1½ x 470g (15-ounce) packaged
    buttercake mix
1 quantity butter cream (page 107)
green food colouring

decorations

90 white Mallow Bakes, halved
30 yellow mini M&M's
candles

1 Preheat oven to 160°C/325°F.
Grease cake pan; line with baking
paper, extending paper 5cm (2 inches)
above sides.
2 Make cake according to directions
on packet. Spread mixture into pan;
bake about 50 minutes. Stand cake
in pan 10 minutes; turn, top-side up,
onto wire rack to cool.
3 Level top of cake, position cake,
cut-side down, on cake board; secure
cake with a little butter cream.
4 Tint three-quarters of the butter
cream pale green; tint remaining butter
cream dark green. Spread pale green
butter cream all over cake.
5 Spoon dark green butter cream into
piping bag; pipe chain around sides of
cake. Using picture as a guide, make
daisies from Mallow Bakes, use mini
M&M's for centres of daisies. Position
candles on cake.

tips You might need to buy two
100g (3-ounce) packets Mallow Bakes.
Use sharp scissors to cut Mallow Bakes
in half. This cake can be made a day ahead.

tips You'll need to buy about three packets of conversation hearts to get 16 pink hearts. This cake can be made a day ahead.

strawberry patch

deep 23cm (9-inch) square cake pan
30cm (12-inch) round or square
    prepared cake board (page 110)
    or plate

cake

1½ x 470g (15-ounce) packaged
    buttercake mix
1 quantity butter cream (page 107)
green food colouring

decorations

16 pink conversation hearts
8 mint leaf lollies, halved lengthways

1 Preheat oven to 150°C/300°F.
Grease cake pan; line base and sides
with baking paper, extending paper
2cm (¾ inch) above sides.
2 Make cake according to directions
on packet. Pour mixture into pan;
bake about 50 minutes. Stand cake
in pan 5 minutes; turn, top-side up,
onto wire rack to cool.
3 Level top of cake, position cake,
cut-side down, on cake board; secure
cake with a little butter cream.
4 Tint remaining butter cream pale
green. Spread all over cake.
5 Using picture as a guide, cut three
slits in each mint leaf half to make
calyx for strawberries. Position calyx
on hearts, cut-side down. Position
strawberries on cake.

coconut-cream layered cake

two deep 20cm (8-inch) round
   cake pans
25cm (10-inch) round prepared cake
   board (page 110) or cake stand
large piping bag fitted with
   small plain tube

light coconut cake

250g (8 ounces) unsalted butter,
   softened
2 teaspoons coconut essence
2 cups (440g) caster (superfine) sugar
1½ cups (375ml) coconut cream
2¼ cups (335g) self-raising flour
6 egg whites
1.25 litres (5 cups) thickened
   (heavy) cream
yellow food colouring

decorations

candles

1 Preheat oven to 160°C/325°F.
Grease cake pans; line base and
side with baking paper, extending
paper 5cm (2 inches) above side.
2 Beat butter, essence and sugar in
small bowl with electric mixer until
light and fluffy. Transfer to large bowl;
stir in coconut cream and sifted flour,
in two batches.
3 Beat egg whites in medium bowl
with electric mixer until soft peaks form.
Fold egg whites into flour mixture,
in two batches.
4 Spread mixture evenly into pans;
bake cakes about 45 minutes. Stand
cakes in pans 5 minutes; turn, top-side
up, onto wire racks to cool.

5 Meanwhile, divide cream between
two medium bowls. Tint one bowl
yellow; leave remaining bowl plain.
Beat both bowls of cream, separately,
with electric mixer until firm peaks form.
6 Split cold cakes in half; layer cakes
with three-quarters of the plain cream
on board or cake stand. Spread cake
all over with yellow cream. Spoon
remaining plain cream into piping
bag; pipe small and large dots over
cake. Position candles on cake;
serve immediately.

tips Cake is best made and assembled on the day. For best piping results, place iced cake and piping bag filled with cream in the refrigerator for about 30 minutes to allow cream to become firm. We found the liquid colouring best for tinting the cream.

tip The cookie dough can be made a day ahead – keep refrigerated. The shoe can be baked a few days ahead – keep in an airtight container. The shoe can be completed the day before the party.

high heel

large oven tray
30cm x 40cm (12-inch x 16-inch)
    rectangular prepared cake board
        (page 110)
small piping bag fitted with
    small plain tube
5cm (2-inch) flower cutter
3cm (1¼-inch) flower cutter

cookie

125g (4 ounces) butter, softened
¾ cup (165g) caster (superfine) sugar
1 egg
1¾ cups (260g) plain (all-purpose) flour
⅓ cup (50g) self-raising flour
1 quantity glacé icing (page 107)
pink and purple food colouring
1 quantity royal icing (page 107)

decorations

30g (1 ounce) ready-made
    white icing (page 107)
1 tablespoon pure icing
    (confectioners') sugar
1 pearl ball

1 To make cookie dough, beat butter, sugar and egg in small bowl with electric mixer until light and fluffy. Transfer mixture to large bowl; stir in sifted flours, in two batches. Knead dough on floured surface until smooth. Cover; refrigerate 30 minutes.
2 Preheat oven to 160°C/325°F. Line oven tray with baking paper.
3 Roll dough between sheets of baking paper until 5mm (¼ inch) thick.
4 Using pattern from pattern sheet, cut out shoe from dough; place on tray. Bake about 25 minutes. Cool on tray.
5 Tint glacé icing purple. Using picture as a guide, and working quickly, spread icing over cookie. Stand until set.
6 Spoon royal icing into piping bag; pipe around edge of shoe. Pipe dots over shoe.

7 Knead ready-made icing on surface dusted with sifted icing sugar until icing loses its stickiness. Divide into two portions; tint one portion pink and the other purple.
8 Roll out icing, one portion at a time, until 5mm (¼ inch) thick. Using large flower cutter, cut shape from pink icing. Using smaller flower cutter, cut shape from purple icing.
9 Using picture as a guide, join flowers using a little royal icing; position pearl ball in centre. Place on shoe.

polka dots

equipment

two deep 23cm (9-inch) round
  cake pans
30cm (12-inch) round prepared cake
  board (page 110) or cake stand
6 small piping bags

vanilla buttercake

250g (8 ounces) unsalted butter,
  softened
2 teaspoons vanilla extract
2½ cups (550g) caster (superfine) sugar
6 eggs
1½ cups (225g) plain (all-purpose) flour
1½ cups (225g) self-raising flour
1 cup (250ml) milk

white chocolate ganache

500g (1 pound) white eating
  chocolate, chopped coarsely
1½ cups (375ml) pouring cream

decorations

315g (10 ounces) white chocolate
  melts, melted
pink, yellow and green food colouring

1 Preheat oven to 140°C/280°F. Grease pans; line base and side with baking paper, extending paper 5cm (2 inches) above side.
2 To make vanilla buttercake, beat ingredients in large bowl on low speed with electric mixer until combined. Increase speed to medium; beat about 2 minutes or until mixture is smooth and changed to a paler colour. Spread mixture evenly between pans; tap gently on bench to release large air bubbles.
3 Bake cakes about 1 hour. Stand cakes in pans 5 minutes; turn, top-side up, onto wire racks to cool.
4 Meanwhile, make white chocolate ganache.
5 Divide melted white chocolate into six small bowls. Use colouring to tint chocolate different shades.
6 Working with one colour at a time, spoon chocolate into piping bags. Pipe small, medium and large discs onto baking-paper-lined tray; tap tray gently on bench to flatten rounds (page 115). Stand at room temperature until set.

7 Sandwich cakes on board or cake stand with one-third of the ganache; spread cake all over with remaining ganache. Decorate with chocolate discs.
white chocolate ganache Stir chocolate and cream in large heatproof bowl over large saucepan of simmering water until smooth. Cover; refrigerate about 3 hours or until thick. Beat ganache in large bowl with electric mixer until firm peaks form.

tips Use small piping bags with or without small plain tubes, or use strong plastic bags – snip a tiny corner from the bag for easy piping. This cake can be made a day ahead; keep in the fridge.

tips You'll need to buy an 80g (2½-ounce) packet of ice-cream wafers, as there will be some breakages when you line and make compartments in the jewellery box. The cake can be completed at least two days ahead.

jewellery box

equipment

deep 20cm (8-inch) square cake pan
20cm (8-inch) square prepared
  cake board (page 110)
30cm (12-inch) square prepared
  cake board (page 110)

cake

470g (15-ounce) packaged
  buttercake mix
1kg (2 pounds) ready-made
  white icing (page 107)
1 cup (160g) pure icing
  (confectioners') sugar
pink food colouring
1 cup (320g) apricot jam (conserve),
  warmed, strained

decorations

10 ice-cream wafers
pearl cachous (dragees)
large and small silver cachous
  (dragees)
square and round jubes
musk Life Savers
pink jelly buttons

1 Preheat oven to 150°C/300°F.
Grease and flour cake pan.
2 Make cake according to directions
on packet. Pour mixture into pan;
bake about 50 minutes. Turn cake,
top-side up, onto wire rack to cool.
3 Knead ready-made icing on surface
dusted with sifted icing sugar until
icing loses its stickiness; tint icing pink.
4 To make lid for the box, brush
underside of smaller cake board with
jam, brush 5cm (2-inch) border of
covered side of board. Stand and
support board on its edge while
preparing the covering. Roll one-
quarter of the icing between sheets
of baking paper, into square shape
large enough to cover the board and
the border underneath. Remove top
piece of baking paper, place board,
bottom-side down onto icing, cut out
the corners of the icing, as if covering
a book with paper; gently fold the icing
over to cover the border on the bottom
of the board. Leave the lid to dry flat on
the baking paper.
5 Level top of cake, position cake,
cut-side down, on larger cake board;
secure with a little jam. Using small
sharp knife, cut a neat square recess

into cake, about 2cm (¾ inch) deep,
leaving a 1cm (½-inch) border around
the edges. Cut the centre piece of the
cake into small squares, cut underneath
each square of cake to remove them.
Brush cake all over with jam.
6 Roll remaining icing on sugared
surface to square shape, large enough
to cover cake. Using rolling pin, lift
icing carefully over cake, allowing for
depth of recess – don't stretch icing.
Using sugared hands, gently ease icing
into corners and sides of recess and
down the sides of the cake. Trim icing
neatly around base of cake (page 112).
7 Before icing sets, line base and sides
of the recess in the box with wafers,
cut with scissors or sharp knife to fit.
Make compartments for box; use small
dabs of jam to hold wafers in place.
8 Using picture as a guide, make
jewellery; use small dabs of jam to
hold jewels in place and to make them
easy to position.
9 Knead some scraps of icing together,
shape into a small cylinder, cut out a
heart-shaped knob for the lid of the
box, secure knob to lid with a little
water or jam. When lid and knob are
set and dry, position lid against box.

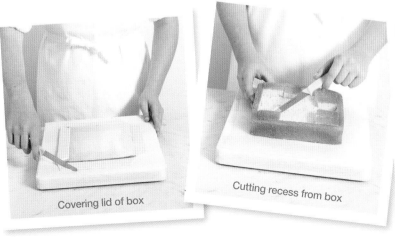

Covering lid of box

Cutting recess from box

Lining box with wafers

castle for a princess

equipment

deep 23cm (9-inch) square cake pan
deep 15cm (6-inch) round cake pan
36cm (14-inch) square prepared
   cake board
2 bamboo skewers

cake

3 x 470g (15-ounce) packaged
   buttercake mix
3 quantities butter cream (page 107)
pink food colouring
2 x 250g (8-ounce) packets vanilla
   creams (biscuits)
5 waffle ice-cream cones
6 ice-cream wafers

decorations

130g (4-ounce) packet candy
   jewellery
4 heart-shaped lollipops
flags
30 sugar cubes
2 pink Mallow Bakes

1 Preheat oven to 130°C/260°F. Grease and flour cake pans.
2 Make cake according to directions on packet. Pour enough mixture into each pan to fill to three-quarters. (Use any leftover mixture to make cupcakes for another occasion). Bake cakes about 1¼ hours. Stand cakes in pans 5 minutes; turn, top-side up, onto wire racks to cool.
3 Tint butter cream pink. Level cake tops, turn square cake, cut-side down onto board (allowing space for drawbridge); secure with a little butter cream. Using one of the biscuits as a guide, cut rounds out of each corner of square cake with a small serrated knife.
4 Secure round cake to square cake with a little butter cream; cover whole cake with butter cream. Stack six biscuits, joining each with butter cream, in each of the cut-out corners of the cake. Using scissors, trim waffle cones to sit flat, position one on each corner and one on the top of the castle to make towers.

5 Remove candy rings from bracelets, position four rings on each lollipop stick, gently push lollipops into each tower; position flags. Position sugar cubes using picture as a guide.
6 Using scissors, trim wafers into shapes for windows, door and drawbridge; position on cake. To make chains for drawbridge: cut skewers to about 12cm (4¾ inches) in length. Position a Mallow Bake at the end of each skewer to hold the candy rings in position. Slide the candy rings onto the skewers; using picture as a guide, position on cake.

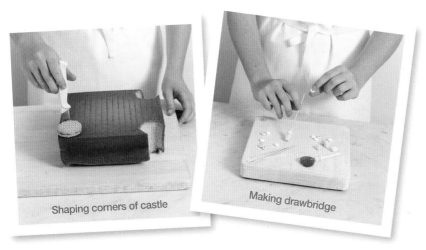

Shaping corners of castle

Making drawbridge

tips Remember to remove the skewers from the drawbridge before cutting the cake. The cake can be completed a day before the party.

fun + games

little cake pops

cardboard egg carton
18 paddle pop sticks

cake

4 cups (340g) firmly packed
    cake crumbs
⅓ cup ready-made (creamy deluxe)
    vanilla frosting
375g (12 ounces) white
    chocolate melts
blue food colouring

decorations

sprinkles

1 Combine cake crumbs and frosting in medium bowl. Roll tablespoons of mixture firmly into balls. Place balls on tray, freeze 1 hour, or refrigerate 3 hours or overnight.
2 Stir chocolate in medium heatproof bowl over medium saucepan of simmering water until smooth (do not allow water to touch bottom of bowl). Transfer one-quarter of the chocolate to a small bowl; tint blue.
3 Meanwhile, stab about 18 small holes, about 5cm (2 inches) apart into top of egg carton. Dip the end of a paddle pop stick into white chocolate, push the stick about half-way into a ball of cake. Repeat with remaining sticks and balls of cake.
4 Swirl cake pops in white chocolate, stand pops upright in egg carton. Refrigerate until chocolate is set.
5 Re-melt blue chocolate if necessary, dip top of pop in blue chocolate, then dip into sprinkles before chocolate is set. Repeat with remaining cake pops and chocolate. Refrigerate pops until ready to serve.
makes 18

tips A quick way to make cake crumbs is to break up a ready-made cake bought from the supermarket. Cake pops can be made and kept in the fridge at least two days before the party. The cake pops become quite firm, and can be placed in a bowl or basket with little or no damage to the pops.

tips You can make it easier on yourself by using a Styrofoam ball instead of cake for the shape of the soccer ball. Position the soccer ball on the cake about an hour before the party. The ball and "field" cakes can be made two days ahead.

soccer ball

1 Preheat oven to 150°C/300°F. Grease round pan; line base and side with baking paper, extending paper 5cm (2 inches) above side. Butter and flour pudding steamers.

2 Make 2 packets of cake mix according to directions on packet. Spread mixture into round pan; bake about 1¼ hours. Stand cake in pan 10 minutes; turn, top-side up onto wire rack to cool.

3 Make remaining cake mix according to directions on packet. Pour mixture evenly into pudding steamers; bake about 40 minutes.

4 Level top of round cake; turn cake, cut-side down, onto cake board; secure cake with a little butter cream. Reserve 1 cup butter cream. Tint remaining butter cream green; spread all over cake.

5 Place coconut and a few drops of green colouring in plastic bag; rub until coconut is evenly coloured. Sprinkle coconut over cake.

6 Trim tops from puddings to make flat. Using small serrated knife, trim cakes to make a 14cm (4¾-inch) diameter ball; join cakes with butter cream. Spread butter cream all over ball.

7 Knead ready-made icing on surface dusted with sifted icing sugar until icing loses its stickiness. Roll two-thirds of the icing until 3mm (⅛ inch) thick. Using hexagon pattern from pattern sheet, cut out 22 shapes. Tint remaining icing black; roll until 3mm (⅛ inch) thick. Using pentagon pattern from pattern sheet, cut out 12 shapes. Using picture as a guide, position shapes onto ball. Place ball on top of cake.

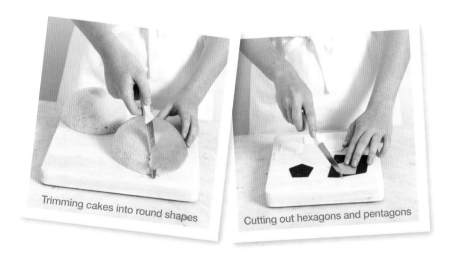

Trimming cakes into round shapes

Cutting out hexagons and pentagons

haunted mountain

equipment

deep 20cm (8-inch) round cake pan
dolly varden cake pan
oven tray
30cm (12-inch) round prepared cake
  board (page 110) or plate

cake

3 x 470g (15-ounce) packaged
  buttercake mix
⅓ cup (110g) apricot jam (conserve),
  warmed, strained
2 quantities fluffy frosting (page 107)

decorations

short 2.5cm (1-inch) diameter candle
marshmallow snow men
1 tablespoon icing (confectioners')
  sugar

1 Preheat oven to 150°C/300°F.
Grease and flour pans.
2 Make cake according to directions
on packet. Pour enough mixture into
round pan until three-quarters full.
Pour enough mixture into dolly varden
pan until 4cm (1½ inches) from top of
pan. Bake both cakes about 1¼ hours.
Stand cakes in pans 5 minutes; turn
cakes, top-side down, onto wire rack
to cool. Turn oven off.
3 Trim tops of both cakes to make flat.
Position round cake, top-side up, on
cake board; secure with a little jam.
Brush cut surface of cake with jam.
Position dolly varden cake, top-side
down, on round cake.
4 Using a small serrated knife, shape
cakes by hollowing out random areas
to give the effect of a rugged mountain.
Position cake on oven tray.

5 Position oven shelves to allow for
the height of the cake. Preheat oven
to 250°C/500°F.
6 Position candle on top of cake,
cover cake with frosting, leaving top
and wick of candle exposed. Bake
cake about 2 minutes or until frosting
is browned lightly.
7 Position snow men on cake.
Dust cake with sifted icing sugar
before serving.

Shaping the mountain

tips Serve the cake as soon as it's browned. If you can't find marshmallow snow men, make your own by joining small and large marshmallows together with a toothpick. Draw faces with an edible cake marker. Make sure you remove toothpicks before serving.

tip This cake can be completed
a day ahead of the party.

alien

deep 12cm (4¾-inch) round cake pan
deep 20cm (8-inch) round cake pan
30cm x 40cm (12-inch x 16-inch)
   rectangular prepared cake board
      (page 110)
12-hole (1-tablespoon/20ml) shallow
   round-based patty pan

cake

1½ x 470g (15-ounce) packaged
   buttercake mix
2 quantities butter cream (page 107)
green and orange food colouring
1 tablespoon apricot jam (conserve),
   warmed, strained

decorations

30g (1 ounce) ready-made
   white icing (page 107)
2 tablespoons pure icing
   (confectioners') sugar
1 orange Skittle
5 TicTacs
2 swirl pops
13 Froot Loops
2 yellow flying saucers

1 Preheat oven to 160°C/325°F. Grease round pans; line base and sides with baking paper, extending paper 5cm (2 inches) above side. Grease one hole of the patty pan.
2 Make cake according to directions on packet. Drop 1 heaped tablespoon mixture into patty pan hole; bake about 20 minutes. Spread 1⅔ cups mixture into small round pan; bake about 45 minutes. Spread remaining mixture into large round pan; bake about 50 minutes. Stand cakes in pans 5 minutes; turn, top-side up, onto wire rack to cool.
3 Tint butter cream pale orange.
4 Trim 2cm (¾-inch) strip from large cake to make top of alien's body. Trim 1cm (½-inch) strip from small cake to make base of alien's head. Shape top edges of cakes to make rounded. Place large cake, cut-side up, on cake board; secure with a little butter cream. Position small cake, cut-side up, on cake board; secure with a little butter cream, joining two flat sides with butter cream. Spread remaining butter cream all over cake.

5 Knead ready-made icing on surface dusted with sifted icing sugar until icing loses its stickiness. Roll out three-quarters of the icing large enough to cover patty cake. Brush rounded side of patty cake with jam, cover cake wtih icing; trim edge. Tint half the remaining icing green; roll out until 3mm (⅛ inch) thick. Cut a 2cm (¾-inch) round from icing; position on patty cake to make eye; position on cake. Position Skittle on eye, secure with a little water. Tint remaining icing orange; shape into mouth, position on cake.
6 Using picture as a guide, decorate cake with TicTacs, lollipops, Froot Loops and flying saucers.

flying ghost

equipment

dolly varden cake pan
deep 20cm (8-inch) round cake pan
6-hole (¾ cup/180ml) texas muffin pan
30cm (12-inch) round prepared
   cake board (page 110)
2 bamboo skewers

cake

3 x 470g (15-ounce) packaged
   buttercake mix
1 cup (320g) apricot jam (conserve),
   warmed, strained
1.5kg (3 pounds) ready-made
   white icing (page 107)
1 cup (160g) pure icing
   (confectioners') sugar

decorations

1 black licorice strap

1 Preheat oven to 150°C/300°F.
Grease and flour cake pans and one
hole of the muffin pan.
2 Make cake according to instructions
on packet. Pour enough mixture into
dolly varden pan until 4cm (1½ inches)
from top of pan. Pour enough mixture
into round pan until three-quarters full.
Pour ½ cup (125ml) mixture into muffin
pan hole.
3 Bake dolly varden cake about
1¾ hours; round cake about 1¼ hours
and muffin, about 30 minutes. Turn
dolly varden cake, top-side down onto
wire rack to cool. Turn remaining cakes,
top-side up, onto wire rack to cool.
4 Level tops of all three cakes to sit
flat. Position round cake, cut-side up,
on board; secure with a little jam, brush
cut surface of cake with a little jam.
Position dolly varden cake, cut-side
down, on top of round cake. Brush
whole cake with jam.

5 To make ghost's arms, cut muffin in
half, from top to bottom. Attach half
a muffin, cut-side down, to each side
of cake, secure with skewers, cut or
broken to right length. Brush arms
with more jam.
6 Knead ready-made icing on surface
dusted with sifted icing sugar, until
icing loses its stickiness. Roll icing
into circle large enough to cover
cake. Using rolling pin, carefully lift
icing over cake, allowing it to drape
over head and arms of ghost. Gently
pull icing into shape around base
of cake, support flounces in icing
with scrunched balls of plastic wrap.
Remove plastic wrap after icing has
become firm.
7 Using scissors, cut licorice into rounds
for eyes and oval shape for mouth,
secure to icing with a dab of jam.
Roll tiny balls of leftover icing for eyes,
secure to licorice with jam.

Attaching arms to ghost

Supporting flounces

tips A metal pudding steamer (2.75 litres/11 cups), could be substituted for the dolly varden pan. Use any leftover cake mixture to make extra cupcakes. This cake can be completed two days ahead of the party, the icing flounces will take overnight to dry.

tips The piñata is quick and easy to make, but make sure the top edge of the shell doesn't have any weak spots. If the piñata does break, re-melt the chocolate and start again. The piñata can be made several days ahead of the party.

piñata

equipment

2.25 litre (9 cup) metal pudding
   steamer
30cm (12-inch) round prepared
   cake board (page 110) or plate

cake

2 teaspoons vegetable oil
375g (12 ounces) white chocolate melts
300g (9½ ounces) chocolate coins
blue and green Smarties

decorations

1 metre (3 feet) ribbon
toy hammer

1 Using fingers, rub oil evenly over inside surface of pudding steamer.
2 Stir chocolate melts in medium heatproof bowl over medium saucepan of simmering water until smooth (do not allow water to touch bottom of bowl). Reserve about a tablespoon of chocolate.
3 Pour remaining chocolate into steamer; swirl to coat inside of steamer evenly. Continue swirling until chocolate begins to set and stops flowing around the steamer; try to keep the chocolate a uniform thickness, particularly at the top edge. Freeze about 20 minutes or until chocolate sets completely.
4 Pile coins in centre of cake board for treasure. Carefully place steamer with set chocolate over coins; using hot cloth, briefly rub outside of steamer. Chocolate shell will slip from steamer to completely enclose coins.
5 Re-melt reserved chocolate; position Smarties, one at a time, on piñata securing with a tiny dab of chocolate.
6 Tie ribbon around piñata, position hammer on board.

Swirling chocolate around steamer

Turning piñata out of steamer

fire engine

equipment

14cm x 21cm (5½-inch x 8½-inch)
   loaf pan
25cm x 30cm (10-inch x 12-inch)
   rectangular prepared cake board
   (page 110)

cake

1½ x 470g (15-ounce) packaged
   buttercake mix
1 quantity butter cream (page 107)
red food colouring

decorations

200g (6½ ounces) ready-made
   white icing (page 107)
¼ cup (40g) pure icing
   (confectioners') sugar
black food colouring
20cm (8-inch) piece black licorice
   strap, halved lengthways
black edible cake marker
4 chocolate cream-filled biscuits
8 Smarties
7 mocha sticks

1 Preheat oven to 150°C/300°F.
Grease and flour pan.
2 Make cake according to directions
on packet. Pour mixture into pan;
bake about 1 hour. Stand cake in pan
5 minutes; turn, top-side up, onto wire
rack to cool.
3 Level top of cake; reserve cake
scraps. Turn cake, cut-side down, onto
surface. Cut into cake at one end to a
depth of about 5mm (¼ inch), for the
windscreen; reserve scraps of cake.
Position scraps of cake on board to
elevate the fire engine slightly; secure
with a little butter cream. Position cake
on cake scraps.
4 Tint butter cream red; spread evenly
all over cake.
5 Knead ready-made icing on surface
dusted with sifted icing sugar until
icing loses its stickiness. Roll out one-
quarter of the icing until 3mm (⅛ inch)
thick. Using patterns from pattern sheet,
cut out windscreen, windows and
number plate. Press windscreen and
windows onto cake.

6 Tint remaining icing grey using black
colouring; roll out until 3mm (⅛ inch)
thick. Cut out one 8cm (3¼-inch)
square and two 3cm x 7cm (1¼-inch x
2¾-inch) rectangles. Using the side of
a metal spatula, make indents, 5mm
(¼ inch) apart, on rectangles to
represent roller doors.
7 Using picture as a guide, position
square on top of fire engine and press
roller doors onto sides. Position licorice
along sides of fire engine. Shape
remaining grey icing into two bumper
bars; position on fire engine. Using
marker, write child's name on number
plate. Attach to bumper bar with a little
butter cream.
8 Using a little butter cream, attach
biscuits to fire engine for wheels. Use
Smarties to make sirens and lights.
Trim mocha sticks to make a ladder
for the roof. Make windscreen wipers
from scraps of licorice.

Shaping windscreen

Making windscreen,
windows and number plate

Making roller doors

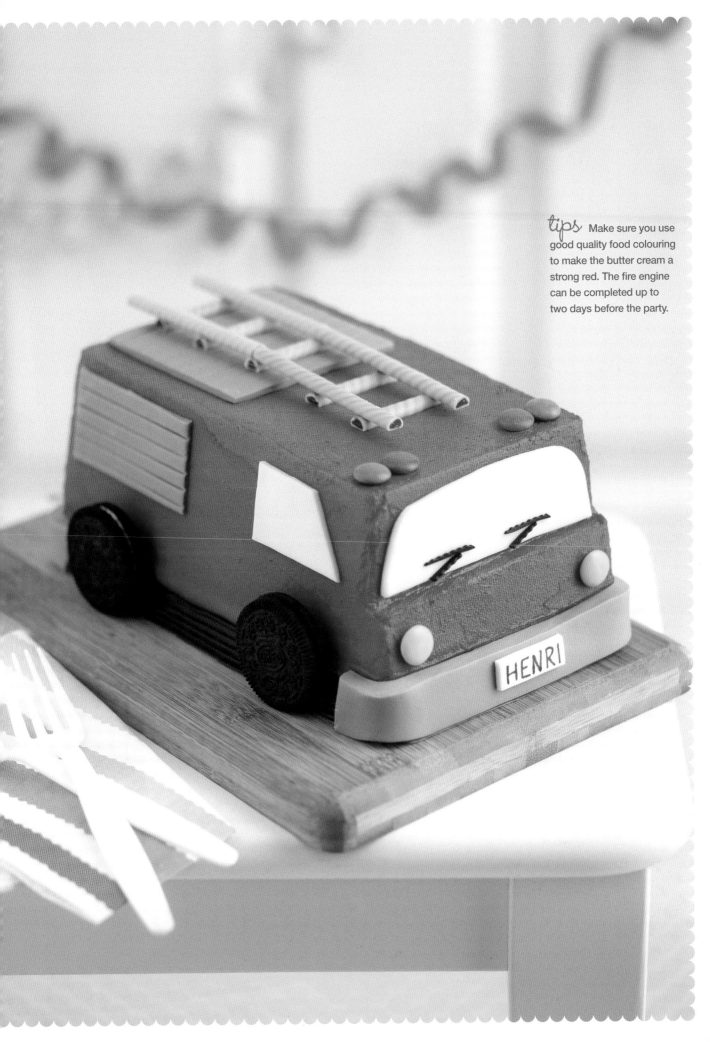

tips Make sure you use
good quality food colouring
to make the butter cream a
strong red. The fire engine
can be completed up to
two days before the party.

HENRI

tip Board shorts can be completed a day before the party.

board shorts

equipment

26cm x 35cm (10¼-inch x 14-inch)
  baking dish
30cm x 40cm (12-inch x 16-inch)
  rectangular prepared cake board
    (page 110)
bamboo skewer

cake

2 x 470g (15-ounce) packaged
  buttercake mix
2 quantities butter cream (page 107)
turquoise and blue food colouring

decorations

90g (3 ounces) ready-made
  white icing (page 107)
2 tablespoons pure icing
  (confectioners') sugar
45cm (18-inch) length polyester cord
5 small yellow jelly beans, halved
33 small white jelly beans

1 Preheat oven to 150°C/300°F.
Grease and flour dish.
2 Make cake according to directions
on packet. Spread mixture into dish;
bake about 50 minutes. Stand cake
in dish 10 minutes; turn, top-side up,
onto wire rack to cool.
3 Level cake top; turn cake cut-side
down. Using pattern from pattern
sheet, cut out shorts; position cake,
cut-side down on cake board, secure
with a little butter cream.
4 Tint butter cream turquoise using
both colourings; spread all over cake.
5 Knead ready-made icing on surface
dusted with sifted icing sugar until
icing loses its stickiness. Roll out to
3mm (⅛ inch) thick. Using pattern from
pattern sheet, cut waistband and two
pockets from icing. Using skewer,
make two holes in centre of waistband;
thread cord through holes and tie
ends in a bow. Position waistband and
pockets on shorts.
6 Using picture as a guide, make
flowers on shorts using jelly beans.

Making waistband

jumbo jet

14cm x 21cm (5½-inch x 8½-inch)
  loaf pan
6-hole texas (¾ cup/180ml)
  muffin pan
30cm (12-inch) square or round
  prepared cake board (page 110)
oven tray

cake

1½ x 470g (15-ounce) packaged
  buttercake mix
1 quantity butter cream (page 107)
blue and grey food colouring

decorations

60g (2 ounces) white chocolate melts,
  melted
2cm (¾-inch) piece black licorice strap
5 ice-cream wafers
candy cake decorations
2 white marshmallows

1 Preheat oven to 150°C/300°F. Grease and flour loaf pan and one hole of the muffin pan.
2 Make cake according to directions on packet. Pour ½ cup mixture into muffin pan hole, pour remaining mixture into loaf pan. Bake muffin about 30 minutes and loaf about 50 minutes. Stand cakes in pans 5 minutes; turn, top-side up, onto wire rack to cool.
3 Level top of loaf cake, turn top-side up, onto board. Using a small serrated knife, trim cake into a rounded shape, slightly pointed at one end.
4 Reserve ½ cup butter cream, tint remaining butter cream blue; secure loaf cake to cake board with a little blue butter cream. Spread blue butter cream all over cake.
5 To make propeller, tint chocolate grey. Using pattern on pattern sheet, make propeller on baking-paper-lined tray. Spread chocolate into propeller shape, tap tray on bench; stand at room temperature until propeller is set. Position propeller and half of one marshmallow, cut-side down on plane.

6 To make cockpit, level top of muffin, turn top-side down onto board, using a serrated knife, cut into a dome shape. Spread rounded side of muffin with reserved butter cream, position cockpit on plane. Position thin strips of licorice for wipers.
7 Using scissors, trim two wafers into large wing shapes. Trim two wafers into smaller wing shapes. Using picture as a guide, position and gently push wings into cake.
8 Trim remaining wafer into shape, rounded at one end for tail fin. Split a marshmallow into three, position two pieces, cut-side down onto tail fin. Attach a candy number to the marshmallows with a little butter cream. Gently push tail fin into cake.

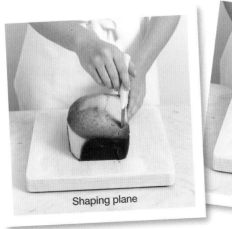

Shaping plane

Shaping wings

tips You need to buy a 80g (2½-ounce) packet of wafers to allow for breakages. The plane and cockpit can be made and covered with butter cream a day ahead. Assemble the plane – particularly the wings – as close to serving as possible.

for little kids

my house

deep 22cm (8¾-inch) square cake pan
30cm (12-inch) square prepared
    cake board (page 110)

cake

1½ x 470g (15-ounce) packaged
    buttercake mix
½ cup (160g) apricot jam (conserve),
    warmed, strained
1kg (2 pounds) ready-made
    white icing (page 107)
½ cup (80g) pure icing
    (confectioners') sugar
blue, red, yellow, brown and
    green food colouring

1 Preheat oven to 150°C/300°F.
Grease pan; line base and sides with
baking paper, extending paper 5cm
(2 inches) above sides.
2 Make cake according to directions
on packet. Spread mixture into pan;
bake about 1 hour. Stand cake in pan
10 minutes; turn, top-side up, onto
wire rack to cool.
3 Level cake top; turn, cut-side down,
onto cake board, secure cake with a
little jam. Brush cake all over with jam.
4 Knead ready-made icing on surface
dusted with sifted icing sugar until icing
loses its stickiness. Roll three-quarters
of the icing into a square large enough
to cover cake. Using rolling pin, lift
icing over cake. Using sugared hands,
smooth icing over cake; trim excess
icing from base of cake (page 112).
5 Divide remaining icing into five
portions; tint each portion a different
suggested colour. Roll each colour, one
at a time, until about 3mm (⅛ inch) thick.
6 Using picture as a guide, cut out
simple shapes from icing using a small
sharp knife. Position icing shapes on
cake; secure with a little jam.

tip Cake can be completed
two days ahead of the party.

tip Cake can be completed a day before the party.

elsie the fish

26cm x 35cm (10¼-inch x 14-inch)
  baking dish
30cm x 40cm (12-inch x 16-inch)
  rectangular prepared cake board
    (page 110)

cake

2 x 470g (15-ounce) packaged
  buttercake mix
1½ quantities butter cream (page 107)
green, blue, orange and purple
  food colourings
125g (4 ounces) ready-made
  white icing (page 107)
½ cup (80g) pure icing
  (confectioners') sugar

decorations

8 white chocolate melts
1 white marshmallow, halved
3 Smarties
5 Froot Loops

1 Preheat oven to 150°C/300°F.
Grease and flour dish.
2 Make cake according to directions
on packet. Spread mixture into dish;
bake about 50 minutes. Stand cake in
dish 10 minutes; turn, top-side down,
onto wire rack to cool.
3 Level top of cake, turn cake, top-
side down. Using pattern from pattern
sheet, cut out fish shape; position
cake on board, secure with a little
butter cream.
4 Tint butter cream aqua using green
and blue colouring; spread butter
cream all over cake.
5 Knead ready-made icing on surface
dusted with sifted icing sugar until icing
loses its stickiness. Tint half the icing
orange; tint remaining icing purple.
Roll both icings, separately, between
sheets of baking paper until about
3mm (⅛ inch) thick.
6 Using pattern from pattern sheet,
cut out shapes from icing. Using
picture as a guide, position shapes
on fish. Push melts into side of cake.
Use slightly squashed marshmallow,
cut-side down, and a Smartie for eye
and two Smarties for lips. Use Froot
Loops for bubbles, securing to board
with a little butter cream.

vegie patch

equipment

deep 15cm (6-inch) square cake pan
20cm (8-inch) square prepared cake
    board (page 110) or cake stand

cake

470g (15-ounce) packaged
    buttercake mix
1 quantity chocolate butter cream
    (page 107)
30g (1 ounce) ready-made
    white icing (page 107)
1 tablespoon pure icing
    (confectioners') sugar
green food colouring

decorations

1 cup (110g) Milo
3 Ferrero Raffaelo white
    chocolate truffles
8 Jaffas
3 orange fruit sticks
3 mint leaf lollies
1 metre (3 feet) ribbon

1 Preheat oven to 150°C/300°F.
Grease cake pan; line with baking
paper, extending paper 5cm (2 inches)
above sides.
2 Make cake according to directions
on packet. Spread mixture into pan;
bake about 55 minutes. Stand cake
in pan 5 minutes; turn, top-side up,
onto wire rack to cool.
3 Level top of cake, turn, cut-side
down, on cake board; secure with a
little butter cream. Spread butter cream
all over cake; sprinkle with Milo.
4 Knead ready-made icing on surface
dusted with sifted icing sugar until icing
loses its stickiness. Tint icing green.
5 Using picture as a guide, shape
small portions of green icing around
each truffle to make cauliflowers;
position cauliflowers in a row on cake.
Roll remaining green icing into thin
sausages; position on cake with Jaffas
to make tomato vine.
6 Cut each fruit stick lengthways into
three; trim to make carrots. Cut mint
leaves, without cutting all the way
through, into thin strips to make carrot
tops. Position bunches of carrots in a
row on cake.
7 Secure ribbon around sides of cake
just before serving.

tips Cauliflowers, carrots and the cake can be made a day ahead of the party. Decorate the cake with Milo, vegies and ribbon about an hour before serving.

tip The cake can be completed – apart from the positioning of the clock's hands – a day ahead of the party.

cute clock

deep 25cm (10-inch) round cake pan
35cm (14-inch) round prepared
    cake board (page 110)
6.5cm (2¾-inch) number cutters

cake

2 x 470g (15-ounce) packaged
    buttercake mix
1 quantity fluffy mock cream frosting
    (page 107)

decorations

200g (6½ ounces) ready-made
    white icing (page 107)
¼ cup (40g) pure icing
    (confectioners') sugar
pink, orange, blue and green
    food colouring
cardboard
silver cachou (dragee)

1 Preheat oven to 150°C/300°F.
Grease pan; line base and sides
with baking paper, extending paper
5cm (2 inches) above sides.
2 Make cake according to directions
on packet. Spread mixture into pan;
bake about 1¼ hours. Stand cake in
pan 10 minutes; turn, top-side up,
onto wire rack to cool.
3 Level cake top; turn cake, cut-side
down, onto cake board, secure with a
little mock cream. Spread remaining
mock cream all over cake.
4 Knead ready-made icing on surface
dusted with sifted icing sugar until icing
loses its stickiness. Divide icing into
four equal portions; tint one portion
pink, one portion orange, one portion
blue and one portion green. Roll each
portion to about 3mm (⅛ inch) thick.
Using cutters, cut out as many
numbers as you like.
5 Using picture as a guide, cut out
hands for clock from cardboard;
position on cake. Position numbers
on cake, side of cake and around
the board.
6 Place a silver cachou in the centre of
cake. Position hands on cachou to lift
hands slightly off the cake's surface.

hoot hoot

deep 20cm (8-inch) square cake pan
30cm (12-inch) square prepared
    cake board (page 110)
small artist's paint brush
small paper piping bag (page 114)

cake

470g (15-ounce) packaged
    buttercake mix
1 quantity butter cream (page 107)
250g (8 ounces) ready-made
    white icing (page 107)
½ cup (80g) pure icing
    (confectioners') sugar
yellow and blue food colouring

decorations

4 white chocolate bullets

1 Preheat oven to 150°C/300°F.
Grease and flour cake pan.
2 Make cake according to directions
on packet. Spread mixture into pan;
bake about 35 minutes. Stand cake in
pan 5 minutes; turn cake, top-side up,
onto wire rack to cool.
3 Meanwhile, tint butter cream yellow.
4 Knead ready-made icing on surface
dusted with sifted icing sugar until
icing loses its stickiness. Roll out about
one-third of the icing between sheets
of baking paper to about 3mm (⅛ inch)
thick; cut out two 2.5cm (1-inch) circles
for whites of eyes. Tint some of the
scraps yellow, roll out between baking
paper; using pattern from pattern
sheet, cut out shape for beak. Tint
remaining icing pale blue, roll between
sheets of baking paper; using pattern
from pattern sheet, cut out shapes
for eyes.
5 Tint scraps and remaining icing a
darker shade of blue, roll between
sheets of baking paper; cut out 1cm
(½-inch) circles for pupils of eyes.
Using pattern from pattern sheet, cut
out wings from remaining icing.

6 Level top of cake; turn, top-side
down. Using pattern from pattern
sheet, cut out owl shape. Position
cake, top-side down, on cake board;
secure with a little butter cream.
7 Reserve 2 tablespoons butter cream,
spread remaining butter cream all
over cake. Using picture as a guide,
position cut out pieces of icing for
eyes, beak and wings. A tiny dab of
water, applied with an artist's brush
to the back of each piece of icing,
will stick the pieces together.
8 Fill piping bag with reserved butter
cream, snip end from bag, pipe tacking
stitches on wings. Position bullets to
form feet.

tips Apart from piping the tacking stitches, the cake can be completed a day ahead of the party. We positioned the owl on a larger cake board decorated with a paper cut-out tree.

tips Use small piping bags with or without small plain tubes, or use strong plastic bags. Snip a tiny corner from the (plastic or paper) bag for easy piping. The cake can be baked two days ahead (or baked and frozen for up to three months). Fill and decorate the cake on the day of serving.

raspberry-layered butterfly cake

two deep 17cm (6¾-inch) round
  cake pans
20cm (8-inch) round prepared cake
  board (page 110) or plate
oven tray
small piping bag

white chocolate cake

185g (6 ounces) white eating
  chocolate, chopped coarsely
90g (3 ounces) unsalted butter,
  chopped coarsely
1 cup (250ml) buttermilk
1¼ cups (275g) caster (superfine) sugar
3 eggs
1 teaspoon vanilla extract
1 cup (150g) plain (all-purpose) flour
½ cup (75g) self-raising flour
½ teaspoon bicarbonate of
  (baking) soda
2 quantities fluffy mock cream
  frosting (page 107)
¼ cup (80g) raspberry jam (conserve),
  warmed, strained, cooled
pink food colouring

decorations

125g (4 ounces) white chocolate
  melts, melted
1.6 metres (5 feet) ribbon,
  approximately

1 Preheat oven to 150°C/300°F.
Grease pans; line base and side
with baking paper, extending paper
5cm (2 inches) above side.
2 Stir chocolate, butter and buttermilk
in medium saucepan over low heat
until smooth. Transfer to large bowl;
cool 10 minutes.
3 Whisk sugar, eggs and extract into
chocolate mixture. Whisk in sifted
dry ingredients until mixture is smooth
and glossy.
4 Divide mixture between pans; bake
about 1 hour. Stand cakes in pans
5 minutes; turn, top-side up, onto wire
racks to cool.
5 Remove half the fluffy mock cream
frosting to a medium bowl, stir in jam;
tint pink.

6 Using pattern from pattern sheet,
trace butterflies onto baking paper
(we used one large, one medium and
five small butterflies); place paper,
marked-side down, onto tray. Tint
melted chocolate pink; spoon into
piping bag. Pipe chocolate around
and inside butterfly shapes on tray;
stand at room temperature until set.
7 Split cold cakes in half; sandwich
cakes with raspberry pink frosting on
cake board. Spread cake all over with
remaining plain frosting. Position
butterflies on cake. Carefully secure
ribbon around cake just before serving.

Piping butterflies

buzzy beehive

equipment

dolly varden pan
30cm (12-inch) round prepared cake
board (page 110) or cake stand

cake

1½ x 470g (15-ounce) packaged
buttercake mix
½ cup (160g) apricot jam (conserve),
warmed, sieved
yellow food colouring

decorations

1.5kg (3 pounds) ready-made
white icing (page 107)
½ cup (80g) pure icing
(confectioners') sugar
1 ice-cream wafer
6 Milo Duos
black decorating gel

1 Preheat oven to 130°C/260°F.
Grease and flour pan.
2 Make cake according to directions
on packet. Pour mixture into pan;
bake about 1 hour. Stand cake in
pan 5 minutes; turn, top-side down,
onto wire rack to cool.
3 Level cake top, position on cake
board; secure with a little jam. Brush
cake all over with jam.
4 Knead ready-made icing on surface
dusted with sifted icing sugar until icing
loses its stickiness; tint icing yellow.
Roll icing into a rope about 1cm (½ inch)
thick and long enough to reach around
the base of cake.
5 Repeat with remaining icing, stacking
ropes up on the cake; keep all the
ropes' joins at the back of the cake.

6 Tint a scrap of icing a darker shade
of yellow; roll into a thin rope. Trim
wafer into a rounded door shape.
Brush around edge of wafer with jam;
attach rope of icing to door.
7 Position door on hive, trace around
door with a knife. Cut door shape out of
icing on cake. Position door on cake.
8 Using picture as a guide, make bees
using remaining icing scraps to shape
bodies, use Milo Duos for wings and
black decorating gel for eyes and
markings. Attach bees to cake with
a little jam.

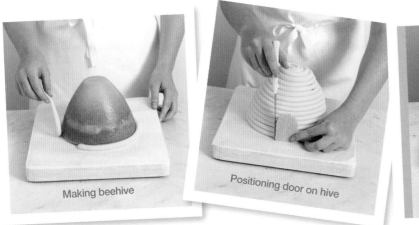

Making beehive

Positioning door on hive

Making bees

tip Cake can be completed two days ahead of the party.

tip The cake can be completed
a day before the party.

tiny town

equipment

26cm x 35cm (10½-inch x 14-inch) baking dish
34cm (13½-inch) square prepared cake board (page 110)
2 small piping bags fitted with small plain tube
small artist's paint brush

cake

3 x 470g (15-ounce) packaged buttercake mix
⅓ cup (50g) white chocolate melts, melted
pink, apricot, green, blue and black food colourings
2 quantities butter cream (page 107)
375g (12 ounces) ready-made white icing (page 107)
⅓ cup (55g) pure icing (confectioners') sugar
⅔ cup (220g) apricot jam (conserve), warmed, strained

decorations

3 ice-cream wafers
yellow sprinkles
4 green lollipops
13 coloured bullets

1 Preheat oven to 150°C/300°F. Grease and flour dish.
2 Make cake according to directions on packet. Spread mixture into dish; bake about 1 hour. Stand cake in dish 10 minutes; turn cake, top-side up, onto wire rack to cool.
3 Meanwhile, make stepping stones: divide chocolate into two small bowls; tint one pink and the other apricot. Spoon pink chocolate into piping bag; pipe small stepping stones onto baking-paper-lined tray (page 115). Tap tray on bench to make stepping stones even. Repeat with apricot chocolate.
4 To make houses, cut a 6cm (2½-inch) slice from the long end of the cake. Cut the slice, crossways into three or four blocks of varying sizes. Refrigerate the houses.
5 Use a small serrated knife to cut some contours into large cake. Position cake cut-side up on cake board; secure with a little butter cream. Colour butter cream pale green; cover cake with butter cream.
6 Knead ready-made icing on surface dusted with sifted icing sugar until icing loses its stickiness. Reserve one-third of the icing for windows, doors, cars and road. Divide remaining icing into three portions; tint one portion pink, one portion apricot and one portion blue.

7 To make houses, brush each house with jam. Roll each coloured portion of icing between sheets of baking paper large enough to cover each house; smooth icing with sugared hands, trim around base of each house neatly. Reserve scraps of coloured icing. Roll out a little of the reserved white icing to make windows and doors, mark window panes with the back of a knife; secure windows and doors to houses with a little jam. Trim wafers with a sharp knife to make rooves; join wafers together and to tops of houses with a little butter cream. Position houses on cake.
8 To make road, tint three-quarters of the remaining reserved icing grey. Roll a narrow strip of icing between sheets of baking paper, long enough to make road. Cut strip of icing to about 2.5cm (1-inch) wide, position on cake. Use sprinkles to mark road, secure each sprinkle to road by brushing a tiny smear of jam onto road's surface.
9 Mould cars from scraps of coloured icing, secure windows and wheels with a little jam. Position cars on road.
10 Decorate cake with stepping stones, lollipops and bullets.

Making houses

Contouring cake

circus tent

equipment

two deep 20cm (8-inch) round
   cake pans
25cm (10-inch) round prepared cake
   board (page 110) or cake stand
plastic ruler

cake

2 x 470g (15-ounce) packaged
   buttercake mix
½ cup (160g) apricot jam (conserve),
   warmed, sieved

decorations

500g (1 pound) ready-made
   white icing (page 107)
½ cup (80g) pure icing
   (confectioners') sugar
40 Kool Mints
flags
candles

1 Preheat oven to 140°C/280°F.
Grease pans; line base and sides
with baking paper, extending paper
5cm (2 inches) above side.
2 Make cake according to directions
on packet. Spread mixture evenly into
pans; bake about 1 hour 10 minutes.
Stand cakes in pan 5 minutes; turn,
top-side up, onto wire racks to cool.
3 Level cake tops; spread cut sides
of cakes with jam. Sandwich cakes,
position on cake board, secure with
a little jam. Spread remaining jam all
over cake.
4 Knead ready-made icing on surface
dusted with sifted icing sugar until
icing loses its stickiness. Divide icing
into four even portions; tint one portion
yellow and one red. Wrap each tightly
in plastic wrap.
5 Roll out one white portion until
large enough to cover top of cake.
Position icing on cake, trim edge
neatly (page 112).

6 Divide remaining white icing into 24
even portions. Knead icing on surface
dusted with icing sugar into 24 x 9cm
(3¾-inch) logs. Repeat with red icing.
Place four logs of each colour side-by-
side, alternating colours; roll logs into a
rectangle about 10cm x 15cm (4 inches
x 6 inches) until 4mm (⅛ inch) thick.
Using ruler as a guide, trim edges of
logs neatly to fit height of cake.
7 Using picture as a guide, press
logs onto side of cake. Repeat with
remaining logs to cover side of cake.
Secure Kool Mints around base of
cake with a little water.
8 To make bunting; roll out yellow icing
until 3mm (⅛ inch) thick. Cut into 3cm
(1¼-inch) triangles; secure around top
edge of cake with a little water.
9 Insert flags and candles into cake.

Making striped pattern

Measuring stripes

Positioning striped icing

tips Keep the ready-made white icing that's not being handled, wrapped tightly in plastic. If logs don't stick together during rolling, brush sides of logs with a little water. The tent can be completed two days ahead of the party.

tips Cake can be made and covered with butter cream a day before the party. Top with popcorn and finish the cake up to three hours before the party. Be sure to remove toothpicks before cutting and serving the cake.

little chicken

equipment

26cm x 35cm (10½-inch x 14-inch) baking dish
35cm (14-inch) square prepared cake board (page 110)

cake

2 x 470g (15-ounce) packaged buttercake mix
1 quantity butter cream (page 107)
yellow, red and orange food colouring

decorations

2 cups (20g) popped popcorn
2 small potato chips (crisps)
1 white marshmallow
1 yellow Skittle
4 ice-cream wafers
50g (1½ ounce) ready-made white icing (page 107)
2 tablespoons pure icing (confectioners') sugar
4 wooden toothpicks

1 Preheat oven to 150°C/300°F. Grease and flour dish.
2 Make cake according to directions on packet. Spread mixture into dish; bake about 50 minutes. Stand cake in dish 10 minutes; turn, top-side up, onto wire rack to cool.
3 Level cake top; turn cake cut-side down. Using pattern from pattern sheet, cut out chicken. Place cake on cake board, cut-side down, secure with a little butter cream.
4 Tint butter cream yellow; spread all over cake.
5 Using picture as a guide, press popcorn onto body of chicken. Gently push chips into cake for beak. Cut marshmallow in half; position, cut-side down, on cake for eye, top with Skittle. Sprinkle two wafers lightly with a little water (this makes it easier to cut) then cut out feet. Gently push into cake.

6 Knead ready-made icing on surface dusted with sifted icing sugar until icing loses its stickiness. Tint red using red and orange colouring; roll out until 3mm (⅛ inch) thick. Using pattern from pattern sheet, cut out comb. Cut two wafers into same shape as comb without trimming the base. Attach icing comb to wafers with a little butter cream. Gently push base of wafers into cake. Secure comb underneath with toothpicks.

Positioning chicken's comb

for big kids

giant donut

equipment

30cm (12-inch) savarin tin
35cm (14-inch) round or square
    prepared cake board (page 110)

cake

4 x 470g (15-ounce) packaged
    buttercake mix
½ cup (160g) strawberry jam
    (conserve), warmed, strained
4½ cups (720g) pure icing
    (confectioners') sugar
⅓ cup (80ml) water, approximately
pink food colouring

decorations

6 yellow and pink musk sticks

1 Preheat oven to 150°C/300°F.
Grease and flour savarin tin.
2 Using two packets cake mix, make
cake according to directions on
packet. Pour mixture into tin; bake
cake about 50 minutes. Stand cake
in tin 5 minutes; turn, top-side down,
onto wire rack to cool. Repeat with
remaining packet mixes.
3 Meanwhile, cut musk sticks into
1cm (½-inch) lengths for sprinkles.
4 Using serrated knife, level tops from
both cakes; spread cut surfaces with
jam. Place one cake, jam-side up,
on cake board; place remaining cake,
jam-side down, on top of bottom cake.
5 To make icing, sift icing sugar into
large heatproof bowl and stir in enough
water to make a stiff paste; tint with
pink colouring. Place bowl over large
saucepan of simmering water, stir
icing until smooth and runny (do not
overheat it or it will crystallise).
6 Quickly pour the icing as evenly as
possible over the cake, avoid using
a spatula if possible. Decorate with
sprinkles immediately before icing sets.

tips Bake one cake at a time, unless you have access to two savarin tins. Have a large metal spatula ready for spreading the icing and the sprinkles close by for decorating; this icing sets rapidly after it has been warmed. If you're not happy with the icing, leave it to set completely, then snap or lift off any ugly pieces on the cake or the board. The cakes can be made and assembled one day ahead. Ice the cake up to an hour before serving.

tips The cake and ice-cream cones can be prepared one day before the party. The frosting is best spread over the cake about an hour before serving. The frosting will lose its gloss after an hour or so.

white Christmas

equipment

deep 20cm (8-inch) round cake pan
30cm (12-inch) round prepared
  cake board (page 110) or plate

cake

1½ x 470g (15-ounce) packaged
  buttercake mix
250g (8 ounces) ready-made
  white icing (page 107)
½ cup (80g) pure icing
  (confectioners') sugar
green food colouring
3 ice-cream waffle cones
¼ cup (80g) apricot jam (conserve),
  warmed, strained
60g (2 ounces) white eating
  chocolate, melted
1 quantity fluffy frosting (page 107)

decorations

5 Ferrero Raffaelo white
  chocolate truffles
silver and pearl
  cachous (dragees)
1 tablespoon icing
  (confectioners') sugar

1 Preheat oven to 150°C/300°F.
Grease cake pan; line base and side,
extending baking paper 5cm (2 inches)
above side.
2 Make cake according to directions
on packet. Spread mixture into pan;
bake about 1¼ hours. Stand cake in
pan 5 minutes; turn, top-side up, onto
wire rack to cool.
3 Knead ready-made icing on surface
dusted with sifted icing sugar until icing
loses its stickiness. Tint icing green;
divide icing into three equal portions.
Roll one portion of icing between
sheets of baking paper into an oval
shape, large enough to wrap around
an ice-cream cone. Brush a cone with
jam, wrap cone in icing. Repeat with
remaining cones, jam and icing. Drizzle
each cone with chocolate; top cones
with silver cachous.
4 Level top of cake; place cake,
top-side down, on cake board, secure
with a little frosting. Spread frosting all
over cake. Position cones, chocolates
and pearl cachous on cake before
frosting sets.
5 Just before serving, dust cake with
sifted icing sugar.

mini mud cake

equipment

two deep 15cm (6-inch) round
cake pans
20cm (8-inch) round prepared cake
board (page 110) or cake stand
2 piping bags fitted with small plain
tube and small fluted tube

milk chocolate mud cake

155g (5 ounces) unsalted butter,
chopped coarsely
125g (4 ounces) milk eating
chocolate, chopped coarsely
1 cup (220g) caster (superfine) sugar
⅔ cup (160ml) milk
2 eggs
1 teaspoon vanilla extract
1 cup (150g) plain (all-purpose) flour
2 tablespoons self-raising flour
2 tablespoons cocoa powder

milk chocolate frosting

1 quantity butter cream (page 107)
90g (3 ounces) milk eating chocolate,
melted, cooled
½ cup (50g) cocoa powder

decorations

1 quantity royal icing (page 107)
blue food colouring
4 blue jelly buttons, halved
candles

1 Preheat oven to 150°C/300°F.
Grease cake pans; line base and side
with baking paper, extending paper
5cm (2 inches) above side.
2 To make milk chocolate mud cake:
stir butter, chocolate, sugar and milk in
medium saucepan over low heat until
smooth. Transfer mixture to large bowl;
cool 10 minutes.
3 Whisk eggs, extract and sifted dry
ingredients into chocolate mixture
until smooth and glossy.
4 Spread mixture into pans; bake
about 1 hour 20 minutes. Stand cakes
in pans 5 minutes; turn, top-side up,
onto wire racks to cool.
5 Meanwhile, make milk chocolate
frosting. Tint royal icing blue.
6 Sandwich cakes together with one-
third of the frosting on cake board.
Spread remaining frosting all over cake.
7 Spoon half the royal icing into piping
bag fitted with plain tube; pipe edging
around base of cake. Spoon remaining
icing into piping bag fitted with fluted
tube; pipe loops around side of cake.
8 Using picture as a guide, position
jelly buttons and candles on cake.

milk chocolate frosting Beat butter
cream in small bowl with electric mixer;
gradually beat in chocolate until
combined. Gradually beat in sifted
cocoa, 1 tablespoon at a time.

Piping shell edging

Piping loops

tips Mud cake can be made two days ahead; store in an airtight container. Assemble and decorate up to six hours ahead of the party.

tips Use any leftover buttercake mix to make cupcakes. The decorated cake can be completed two days ahead of the party. Tracing wheels are available from the haberdashery section of most chainstores. You could also use fabric ribbon instead of making your own out of ready-made white icing.

present cake

equipment

deep 15cm (6-inch) round cake pan
deep 23cm (9¼-inch) square cake pan
15cm (6-inch) round prepared
  cake board (page 110)
30cm (12-inch) square prepared
  cake board (page 110)
2 medium piping bags fitted with
  medium plain tubes
tracing wheel
3 bamboo skewers

cake

3 x 470g (15-ounce) packaged
  buttercake mix
½ cup (160g) apricot jam (conserve),
  warmed, sieved
blue, yellow and pink food colouring
1 quantity royal icing (page 107)

decorations

1.5kg (3 pounds) ready-made
  white icing (page 107)
½ cup (80g) pure icing
  (confectioners') sugar

1 Preheat oven to 150°C/300°F. Grease and flour pans.

2 Make cake according to directions on packet. Pour mixture into pans until each is three-quarters full; bake round cake 1 hour and square cake about 1¼ hours. Stand cakes in pans 10 minutes; turn, top-side up, onto wire rack to cool.

3 Level cakes to the same height; turn round cake, cut-side down, onto small cake board. Turn square cake, cut-side down onto large cake board. Secure cakes to boards with a little jam. Brush cakes all over with jam.

4 Knead ready-made icing on surface dusted with sifted icing sugar until icing loses its stickiness.

5 Tint two-thirds of the icing blue. Roll icing on sugared surface until large enough to cover square cake. Using rolling pin, lift icing over cake; smooth with sugared hands. Trim neatly around base (page 112).

6 Reserve an apple-sized piece of icing for bow. Tint remaining icing yellow. Roll icing to a round shape large enough to cover round cake. Using rolling pin, lift icing over cake; smooth with sugared hands. Trim neatly around base (page 112).

7 Insert trimmed bamboo skewers into centre of square cake to support round cake (page 115). Position round cake (still on its cake board) on skewers.

8 Tint half the royal icing yellow, tint remaining icing pink. Spoon yellow royal icing into one of the piping bags, pipe dots around square cake. Spoon pink icing into remaining piping bag, pipe dots around round cake.

9 Tint reserved icing pink. Roll out icing to about 20cm x 45cm (8 inches x 18 inches) and 4mm (¼ inch) thick; cut into three strips. Using picture as a guide, use a tracing wheel to mark edges of ribbon.

10 Turn two of the strips over, brush lightly with water. Using picture as a guide, drape damp side of strips over cakes.

11 Cut remaining strip in half, fold into bow shapes, join loops with water. Place shapes on their sides on baking-paper-lined tray; stand overnight to dry. Reserve scraps. Position bow shapes on cake; use a scrap of icing to make middle of bow.

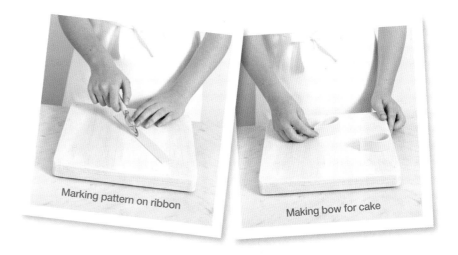

Marking pattern on ribbon

Making bow for cake

topsy turvy cake

equipment

deep 9cm (3¾-inch) square cake pan
deep 15cm (6-inch) square cake pan
deep 23cm (9¼-inch) square cake pan
30cm (12-inch) square prepared cake
    board (page 110) or cake stand

cake

5 x 470g (15-ounce) packaged
    buttercake mix
2½ quantities butter cream (page 107)
blue food colouring

decorations

300g (9½ ounces) ready-made
    white icing (page 107)
¼ cup (40g) pure icing
    (confectioners') sugar
15 white chocolate melts
8 silver cachous (dragees)
candles

1 Preheat oven to 150°C/300°F. Grease pans; line base and sides with baking paper, extending paper 5cm (2 inches) above sides.

2 Make cake according to directions on packet (see tip). Spread 1½ cups mixture into small pan; 4 cups mixture into medium pan and remaining mixture into large pan. Bake small cake about 1¼ hours; medium cake about 1¾ hours and large cake about 2 hours. Stand cakes in pans 5 minutes; turn, top-side up, onto wire rack to cool.

3 Level cake tops; trim cakes on an angle.

4 Place large cake, cut-side up, on cake board; secure with a little butter cream. Reserve 1½ cups butter cream; tint blue. Spread three-quarters of the remaining plain butter cream all over large cake.

5 Place medium cake, cut-side down, at a slight angle in centre of large cake. Spread blue butter cream all over medium cake. Position small cake, cut-side down, on medium cake. Spread remaining butter cream all over cake.

6 Knead ready-made icing on surface dusted with sifted icing sugar until icing loses its stickiness. Roll icing until 3mm (⅛ inch) thick. Cut into 1cm (½-inch) strips, long enough to make stripes about 1.5cm (¾-inch) apart on the sides of the large cake.

7 Using picture as a guide, use white chocolate melts (some halved) to decorate middle cake.

8 Roll remaining icing until 3mm (⅛ inch) thick. Cut out four 5mm (¼-inch) curved, slightly tapered strips; position on each side of top cake. Position cachous on each corner. Position candles.

Cutting cakes on an angle

tips Make buttercake mixes in batches as they will not all fit together in a large bowl: use three packets first, then remaining two packets. The tiers of this cake are not supported by skewers so it's important to use a light cake such as a buttercake or packet mix, and to assemble the cake up to about four hours before the party.

tips Ice-cream cake and cookies can be prepared one day ahead. Store cookies in an airtight container. Use regular ice-cream for best results – high or low fat ice-creams are not suitable. Assemble cake just before serving. Use a serrated knife to cut the cake.

choc-chip ice-cream sandwich

equipment

two deep 23cm (9¼-inch) round
  cake pans
25cm (10-inch) round prepared
  cake board (page 110) or plate
oven tray

cake

4 litres (16 cups) vanilla ice-cream
125g (4 ounces) unsalted butter,
  softened
1 teaspoon vanilla extract
⅓ cup (55g) caster sugar
⅓ cup (55g) firmly packed light
  brown sugar
1 egg
1 cup (150g) plain (all-purpose) flour
¾ cup (110g) self-raising flour
½ cup (95g) dark Choc Bits
10 dark chocolate melts

1 Line one cake pan with four layers
of plastic wrap, extending plastic wrap
10cm (4 inches) over side of pan.
2 Working quickly, spoon ice-cream
into pan, pressing down firmly and
smoothing surface. Fold plastic wrap
over ice-cream to enclose. Freeze
3 hours or overnight until firm.
3 Remove ice-cream from pan, still
wrapped in plastic; place on oven tray.
Return to freezer.
4 Preheat oven to 150°C/300°F.
Grease both cake pans.
5 Beat butter, extract and sugars in
small bowl with electric mixer until light
and fluffy. Beat in egg until combined.
Transfer mixture to large bowl; stir in
sifted flours then Choc Bits.

6 Divide dough in half; press one half
over base of pan. Press remaining
half over base of second pan, leaving
1cm (½-inch) gap around edge of
dough; push chocolate melts onto
top of dough.
7 Bake cookies about 20 minutes.
Stand in pans 20 minutes; turn,
top-side up, onto wire racks to cool.
8 Place plain cookie on cake board;
top with ice-cream cake then choc-
topped cookie. Serve immediately.

Preparing cookies

box of popcorn

equipment
deep 23cm (9¼-inch) square cake pan
30cm (12-inch) square prepared
  cake board (page 110)

cake
2 x 470g (15-ounce) packaged
  buttercake mix
1 quantity butter cream (page 107)
blue colouring

decorations
500g (1 pound) ready-made
  white icing (page 107)
½ cup (80g) pure icing
  (confectioners') sugar
blue writing icing
1½ cups (15g) popped popcorn

1 Preheat oven to 150°C/300°F. Grease pan; line base and sides with baking paper, extending paper 5cm (2 inches) above sides.
2 Make cake according to directions on packet. Spread mixture into pan; bake about 1 hour. Stand cake in pan 10 minutes; turn, top-side up, onto wire rack to cool.
3 Level cake top to make cake about 5cm (2 inches) high; turn cake cut-side down. Using pattern from pattern sheet, cut out popcorn box. Place cake on cake board, cut-side down, secure with a little butter cream. Spread butter cream all over cake.

4 Knead ready-made icing on surface dusted with sifted icing sugar until icing loses its stickiness. Divide icing in half. Tint one half blue; roll out to 3mm (⅛ inch) thick. Cut into 1.5cm (¾-inch) strips. Repeat making strips with other half of icing.
5 Using picture as a guide, position strips along sides and top of cake, trimming and tapering slightly to fit the bottom of the popcorn box. Roll out scraps of white icing. Cut icing into a 3cm x 5cm (1¼-inch x 2-inch) rectangle. Position on box with a little butter cream; write child's name with writing icing.
6 Press popcorn gently onto butter cream up to an hour before serving.

Cutting strips to size

Position strips on cake

tips Cake can be made and decorated with strips and label a day ahead of the party. Write the child's name on the label and position the popcorn an hour before serving.

tips Cake and ganache can be made a day ahead. Store cake in an airtight container. Whip ganache and assemble layered cake up to an hour before serving.

chocolate cake

equipment

two deep 20cm (8-inch) round
   cake pans
25cm (10-inch) round prepared cake
   board (page 110) or cake stand

devil's food cake

185g (6 ounces) dark eating
   chocolate, chopped coarsely
⅓ cup (35g) cocoa powder
1⅔ cups (410ml) boiling water
250g (8 ounces) unsalted butter,
   softened
2 cups (220g) firmly packed
   dark brown sugar
4 eggs
1 teaspoon vanilla extract
¾ cup (180g) sour cream
1 cup (150g) plain (all-purpose) flour
1 cup (150g) self-raising flour
1 teaspoon bicarbonate of
   (baking) soda

milk chocolate ganache

700g (1½ pounds) milk eating
   chocolate, chopped coarsely
1⅔ cups (410ml) pouring cream

decorations

candles

1 Preheat oven to 140°C/280°F.
Grease cake pans: line base and
sides with baking paper.
2 Stir chocolate, sifted cocoa and the
water in medium saucepan over low
heat until smooth. Transfer mixture to
large bowl; cool 15 minutes.
3 Add butter, sugar, eggs, extract,
sour cream and sifted dry ingredients
to chocolate mixture; beat on low speed
with electric mixer until combined.
Increase speed to medium; beat about
3 minutes or until mixture is smooth
and changed to a paler colour.
4 Spread mixture into pans; bake
about 1¼ hours. Stand cakes in pans
5 minutes; turn, top-side up, onto wire
racks to cool.
5 Meanwhile, make milk chocolate
ganache.

6 Split cakes in half; sandwich cakes
using about ½ cup of the ganache
between each layer. Position cake
on cake board, secure with a little
ganache. Spread cake all over with
remaining ganache. Position candles
on cake.
milk chocolate ganache Combine
ingredients in large heatproof bowl over
large saucepan of simmering water; stir
until smooth. Cover; refrigerate about
3 hours or until thick. Beat ganache
in large bowl with electric mixer until
firm peaks form.

sea shell cake

equipment

two 20cm (8-inch) round cake pans
30cm (12-inch) round prepared
   cake board (page 110) or plate
shell-shaped chocolate moulds

cake

2 x 470g (15-ounce) packaged
   buttercake mix
2 quantities butter cream (page 107)

decorations

375g (12 ounces) white
   chocolate melts
yellow food colouring
½ cup (40g) desiccated
   coconut, toasted
45 pearl balls
candles

1 Preheat oven to 150°C/300°F.
Grease and flour pans.
2 Make cake according to directions
on packet. Spread mixture evenly
between pans; bake about 50 minutes.
Stand cakes in pans 5 minutes; turn,
top-side up, onto wire racks to cool.
3 Stir chocolate in medium heatproof
bowl over medium saucepan of
simmering water (do not allow water
to touch base of bowl) until melted.
Pour half the chocolate into shell
moulds. Tint remaining chocolate
yellow; pour into remaining moulds.
Refrigerate until set.
4 Level cake tops, spread cut side of
cakes with some of the butter cream;
sandwich cakes. Position cake on
cake board, secure with a little butter
cream. Spread remaining butter cream
all over cake.
5 Using picture as a guide, position
chocolate shells around cake. Sprinkle
with toasted coconut. Decorate cake
with pearl balls and candles.

Making chocolate shells

tip Cake can be completed a day ahead of the party.

numbers

one

26cm x 35cm (10½-inch x 14-inch)
   baking dish
30cm x 40cm (12-inch x 16-inch)
   rectangular prepared cake board
      (page 110) or plate
plastic ruler
small piping bag fitted with
   small plain tube

cake

2 x 470g (15-ounce) packaged
   buttercake mix
⅓ cup (110g) apricot jam (conserve),
   warmed, strained
500g (1 pound) ready-made
   white icing (page 107)
½ cup (80g) pure icing
   (confectioners') sugar
ivory food colouring
1 quantity royal icing (page 107)

1 Preheat oven to 150°C/300°F.
Grease and flour dish.
2 Make cake according to directions
on packet. Spread mixture into dish;
bake about 50 minutes. Stand cake
in dish 10 minutes; turn, top-side up,
onto wire rack to cool.
3 Level top of cake. Turn cake, cut-
side down. Using sharp serrated knife
and pattern from pattern sheet, cut out
number one shape. Position cake on
board, secure with a little jam. Brush
cake all over with jam.
4 Knead ready-made icing on surface
dusted with sifted icing sugar until
icing loses its stickiness; tint ivory.

5 Roll icing on sugared surface until
large enough to cover cake. Using
rolling pin, lift icing onto cake; smooth
icing with sugared hands. Trim icing
neatly around base of cake (page 112).
6 Use edge of ruler to mark diagonal
quilting pattern on icing before it sets
and develops a crust.
7 Fill piping bag with about half the
royal icing (use remaining icing to
decorate other cakes for the party).
Using picture as a guide, pipe dots
where lines cross.

Marking quilting pattern

Piping dots on quilting

tips The dots on the quilting
can be piped before or after the
covering icing has set. The cake
can be completed up to three
days before the party.

tips We found it easier to cover half the cake at a time with ready-made icing. This stage can be done up to two days ahead of the party. Complete the cake up to four hours before the party.

two

equipment

26cm x 35cm (10½-inch x 14-inch)
  baking dish
30cm x 40cm (12-inch x 16-inch)
  rectangular prepared cake board
    (page 110)

cake

2 x 470g (15-ounce) packaged
  buttercake mix
⅓ cup (110g) apricot jam (conserve),
  warmed, strained
900g (1¾ pounds) ready-made
  white icing (page 107)
½ cup (80g) pure icing
  (confectioners') sugar
blue food colouring
½ quantity glacé icing (page 107)

decorations

½ cup (2 sachets) sprinkles

1 Preheat oven to 150°C/300°F.
Grease and flour dish.
2 Make cake according to directions
on packet. Spread mixture into dish;
bake about 50 minutes. Stand cake
in dish 10 minutes; turn, top-side up,
onto wire rack to cool.
3 Level cake top; turn cake, cut-side
down. Using pattern from pattern
sheet, cut out number two from cake.
Position cake on cake board, brush
cake all over with jam.
4 Knead ready-made icing on surface
dusted with sifted icing sugar until
icing loses its stickiness; tint pale
blue. Roll out half the icing until 5mm
(¼ inch) thick. Using rolling pin, lift
icing over bottom half of cake. Using
sugared hands, mould icing over top
and sides of cake; trim neatly around
base (page 112).
5 Repeat with remaining icing for
top half of cake, carefully joining in
the middle.
6 Tint glacé icing a darker blue than
the icing on the cake. Using picture as
a guide, and working quickly, spread
glacé icing over cake. Decorate cake
with sprinkles immediately, before
icing sets.

Covering the cake

three

26cm x 35cm (10½-inch x 14-inch)
  baking dish
30cm x 40cm (12-inch x 16-inch)
  rectangular prepared cake board
  (page 110)
7cm (2¾-inch) round cutter

cake

2 x 470g (15-ounce) packaged
  buttercake mix
1 quantity fluffy frosting (page 107)
pink food colouring

decorations

16 white chocolate melts

1 Preheat oven to 150°C/300°F.
Grease and flour dish.
2 Make cake according to directions
on packet. Spread mixture into dish;
bake about 50 minutes. Stand cake
in dish 10 minutes; turn, top-side up,
onto wire rack to cool.
3 Level cake top; turn cake cut-side
down. Using pattern from pattern
sheet, cut number three from cake.
4 Position cake on cake board; secure
with a little frosting. Tint fluffy frosting
pink; spread all over cake.
5 Using cutter cut through about half of
the chocolate melts to make the edges
of the melts rounded. Using picture as
a guide, decorate cake with melts.

tips To keep the glossy finish to the frosting, the cake needs to be frosted up to an hour before the party. The frosting soon dries out to resemble cooked meringue.

tips To keep the glossy finish to the frosting, the cake needs to be frosted up to an hour before the party. The frosting soon dries out to resemble cooked meringue.

four

equipment

26cm x 35cm (10½-inch x 14-inch)
    baking dish
30cm x 40cm (12-inch x 16-inch)
    rectangular prepared cake board
        (page 110)

cake

2 x 470g (15-ounce) packaged
    buttercake mix
1 quantity fluffy frosting (page 107)
orange, yellow, blue, green and
    pink food colouring

decorations

small paint brush

1 Preheat oven to 150°C/300°F.
Grease and flour dish.
2 Make cake according to directions
on packet. Spread mixture into dish;
bake about 50 minutes. Stand cake
in dish 10 minutes; turn, top-side up,
onto wire rack to cool.
3 Level cake top; turn cake cut-side
down. Using pattern from pattern
sheet, cut number four from cake.
4 Position cake on cake board; secure
with a little fluffy frosting. Reserve 1 cup
frosting; spread remaining frosting all
over cake.
5 Divide reserved frosting into five
small bowls; tint each bowl with one
of the suggested colours – orange,
yellow, blue, green and pink.
6 Using picture as guide, dollop
spoonfuls of coloured frosting onto
cake; position paint brush on cake.

five

equipment

3cm (1¼-inch) five-pointed star cutter
5cm (2-inch) six-pointed star cutter
eight 10cm (4-inch) lengths
  florists' wire
oven tray
26cm x 35cm (10½-inch x 14-inch)
  baking dish
30cm x 40cm (12-inch x 16-inch)
  rectangular prepared cake board
    (page 110)

cake

2 x 470g (15-ounce) packaged
  buttercake mix
1½ quantities butter cream (page 107)
yellow food colouring

decorations

200g (6½ ounces) ready-made
  white icing (page 107)
2 tablespoons pure icing
  (confectioners') sugar
blue food colouring

1 Knead ready-made icing on surface dusted with sifted icing sugar until icing loses its stickiness; divide icing in half. Tint one portion blue; tint remaining portion dark blue. Roll out each colour, one at a time, until 5mm (¼ inch) thick. Using both star cutters, cut out star shapes from both icings.

2 Using picture as a guide, bend and curl lengths of florists' wire. Wet one end of each length of wire; push damp ends into sides of some of the smaller stars. Place on baking-paper-lined tray; stand overnight to dry.

3 Preheat oven to 150°C/300°F. Grease and flour dish.

4 Make cake according to directions on packet. Spread mixture into dish; bake about 50 minutes. Stand cake in dish 10 minutes; turn, top-side up, onto wire rack to cool.

5 Level top of cake; turn cake cut-side down. Using pattern from pattern sheet, cut number five from cake. Position cake, cut-side down, on cake board; secure with a little butter cream.

6 Tint butter cream yellow; spread all over cake.

7 Using picture as a guide, position stars on cake.

Wiring stars

tips While the stars need to be made a day ahead to dry, the cake can also be made and covered with butter cream the day before to make it easier on party day. Decorate the cake with stars up to three hours before the party.

tip The cake can be completed a day before the party.

six

equipment

26cm x 35cm (10½-inch x 14-inch)
   baking dish
30cm x 40cm (12-inch x 16-inch)
   rectangular prepared cake board
   (page 110)

cake

2 x 470g (15-ounce) packaged
   buttercake mix
2 quantities butter cream (page 107)
purple food colouring

decorations

125g (4 ounces) ready-made
   white icing (page 107)
2 tablespoons pure icing
   (confectioners') sugar
yellow food colouring
1 white marshmallow, halved
22 yellow Smarties
36 purple Smarties
5cm (2-inch) piece black
   licorice strap

1 Preheat oven to 150°C/300°F.
Grease and flour dish.
2 Make cake according to directions
on packet. Spread mixture into dish;
bake about 50 minutes. Stand cake
in dish 10 minutes; turn, top-side up,
onto wire rack to cool.
3 Level top of cake; turn cake cut-
side down. Using pattern from pattern
sheet, cut number six from cake.
Cut through the number six as shown
below, trim and shape the cake to
make the snake's head. Position
cake, cut-side down, on cake board;
secure with a little butter cream.
4 Tint three-quarters of the butter
cream purple; spread all over cake,
leaving the snake's head plain. Tint
remaining butter cream dark purple;
spread over snake's head.

5 Knead ready-made icing on surface
dusted with sifted icing sugar until
icing loses its stickiness; tint yellow.
Divide icing into five portions; roll each
portion into a 5mm (¼-inch) rope.
Using picture as a guide, position
ropes across snake's body, trim ends.
6 Using picture as a guide, position
marshmallows, cut-side up, for eyes;
top each with a yellow Smartie.
Position remaining Smarties across
snake's body to represent bands. Cut a
small triangle from one end of licorice,
position for snake's tongue.

Shaping snake's head

seven

26cm x 35cm (10½-inch x 14-inch)
   baking dish
30cm x 40cm (12-inch x 16-inch)
   rectangular prepared cake board
   (page 110)

cake

2 x 470g (15-ounce) packaged
   buttercake mix
1 quantity fluffy frosting (page 107)

decorations

14 ready-made yellow and white
   sugar flowers

1 Preheat oven to 150°C/300°F.
Grease and flour dish.
2 Make cake according to directions
on packet. Spread mixture into dish;
bake about 50 minutes. Stand cake
in dish 10 minutes; turn, top-side up,
onto wire rack to cool.
3 Level top of cake; turn cake cut-side
down. Using pattern from pattern
sheet, cut number seven from cake.
4 Meanwhile, make fluffy frosting.
5 Position cake, cut-side down, on
cake board; secure with a little frosting.
6 Spread remaining frosting all over
cake. Using picture as a guide, position
flowers on cake.

tips To keep the glossy finish to the frosting, the cake needs to be frosted up to an hour before the party. The frosting soon dries out to resemble cooked meringue.

tip Cake can be completed
a day before the party.

eight

equipment

26cm x 35cm (10½-inch x 14-inch)
  baking dish
50cm (20-inch) round prepared
  cake board (page 110)
small piping bag fitted with
  small plain tube

cake

2 x 470g (15-ounce) packaged
  buttercake mix
2 quantities butter cream (page 107)
yellow food colouring
1 teaspoon cocoa powder

decorations

1 toy train
3 lollipops
flags

1 Preheat oven to 150°C/300°F.
Grease and flour dish.
2 Make cake according to directions
on packet. Spread mixture into dish;
bake about 50 minutes. Stand cake
in dish 10 minutes; turn, top-side up,
onto wire rack to cool.
3 Level cake top; turn cake, cut-side
down. Using pattern from pattern sheet,
cut number eight from cake. Position
cake, cut-side down on cake board.
4 Reserve ½ cup butter cream. Tint
remaining butter cream yellow; spread
all over cake.
5 Stir sifted cocoa into reserved butter
cream; spoon into piping bag. Using
picture as a guide, pipe chocolate
butter cream onto cake to make train
tracks. Position train, lollipops and
flags on cake.

nine

equipment

26cm x 35cm (10½-inch x 14-inch)
  baking dish
30cm x 40cm (12-inch x 16-inch)
  rectangular prepared cake board
  (page 110)

cake

2 x 470g (15-ounce) packaged
  buttercake mix
1 quantity fluffy frosting (page 107)
orange food colouring

decorations

2 x 130g (4-ounce) packets
  candy jewellery

1 Preheat oven to 150°C/300°F.
Grease and flour dish.
2 Make cake according to directions
on packet. Spread mixture into dish;
bake about 50 minutes. Stand cake
in dish 10 minutes; turn, top-side up,
onto wire rack to cool.
3 Level top of cake; turn cake cut-
side down. Using pattern from pattern
sheet, cut number nine from cake.
4 Position cake, cut-side down, on
cake board; secure with a little fluffy
frosting.
5 Tint frosting orange; spread all over
cake. Using picture as a guide, position
candy jewellery on cake.

tips To keep the glossy finish to the frosting, the cake needs to be frosted up to an hour before the party. The frosting soon dries out to resemble cooked meringue.

cake recipes

If you want to make your own cakes, these recipes will all bake at similar temperatures, times, and in the same pan sizes as the packet mix cakes suggested in each recipe. One quantity of each of these cake recipes is equivalent to one 470g (15-ounce) packaged cake mix.

Basic buttercake

125g (4 ounces) butter, softened
½ teaspoon vanilla extract
¾ cup (165g) caster (superfine) sugar
2 eggs
1½ cups (225g) self-raising flour
½ cup (125ml) milk

Preheat oven. Grease (and line) pan(s). Beat butter, extract and sugar in small bowl with electric mixer until light and fluffy. Beat in eggs, one at a time. Stir in sifted flour and milk, in two batches. Bake as directed.
To marble a buttercake, place portions of cake mixture in three bowls then tint each with the desired colours. Drop spoonfuls of mixture into pan(s), alternating colours, then swirl together with a skewer for a marbled effect.

Quick chocolate cake

1⅓ cups (200g) self-raising flour
½ cup (50g) cocoa powder
125g (4 ounces) butter, softened
½ teaspoon vanilla extract
1¼ cups (275g) caster
   (superfine) sugar
2 eggs
⅔ cup (160ml) water

Preheat oven. Grease (and line) pan(s). Sift flour and cocoa into medium bowl, add remaining ingredients; beat on low speed with electric mixer until ingredients are combined. Increase speed to medium; beat about 3 minutes or until mixture is smooth and changed to a lighter colour. Bake as directed.

White chocolate mud cake

165g (5 ounces) butter,
   chopped coarsely
100g (3 ounces) white eating
   chocolate, chopped coarsely
1 cup (220g) caster (superfine) sugar
⅔ cup (160ml) milk
1 cup (150g) plain (all-purpose) flour
⅓ cup (50g) self-raising flour
1 egg

Preheat oven. Grease (and line) pan(s). Combine butter, chocolate, sugar and milk in medium saucepan; stir over low heat until smooth. Cool 30 minutes. Whisk in sifted flours, then egg. Bake as directed.

Dark chocolate mud cake

225g (7 ounces) butter,
   chopped coarsely
360g (11½ ounces) dark chocolate,
   chopped coarsely
¾ cup (165g) firmly packed
   brown sugar
¾ cup (180ml) water
1 cup (150g) plain (all-purpose) flour
¼ cup (35g) self-raising flour
2 tablespoons cocoa powder
2 eggs

Preheat oven. Grease (and line) pan(s). Combine butter, chocolate, sugar and the water in medium saucepan; stir over low heat until smooth. Cool 30 minutes. Whisk in sifted flours and cocoa, then eggs. Bake as directed.

Carrot cake

½ cup (125ml) vegetable oil
2 eggs
¾ cup (110g) self-raising flour
½ cup (110g) firmly packed brown sugar
2 teaspoons mixed spice
1½ cups (360g) firmly packed
   coarsely grated carrot

Preheat oven. Grease (and line) pan(s). Combine oil, eggs, sifted flour, sugar and spice in medium bowl; stir in carrot. Bake as directed.

Gluten-free buttercake

100g (3 ounces) butter, softened
1 cup (150g) gluten-free
   self-raising flour
½ cup (110g) caster (superfine) sugar
¼ cup (60ml) milk
1 egg
1 egg white

Preheat oven. Grease (and line) pan(s). Beat butter in small bowl with electric mixer until changed to a paler colour. Sift flour and 2 tablespoons of the sugar together. Beat flour mixture and milk into the butter, in two batches until combined. Beat egg and egg white in small bowl with electric mixer until thick and creamy. Gradually add remaining sugar, beating until sugar dissolves. Gradually pour egg mixture into flour mixture with motor operating on a low speed, only until combined. Bake as directed.

Gluten-free carrot cake

1 cup (125g) soy or besan
   (chickpea) flour
¾ cup (110g) 100% corn cornflour
   (cornstarch)
2 teaspoons gluten-free
   baking powder
1 teaspoon bicarbonate of
   (baking) soda
2 teaspoons mixed spice
1 cup (220g) firmly packed
   brown sugar
1 cup (120g) coarsely chopped
   roasted walnuts
1½ cups (360g) coarsely grated carrot
½ cup (125ml) extra light olive oil
½ cup (120g) sour cream
3 eggs

Preheat oven. Grease (and line) pan(s). Sift flours, baking powder, soda and spice into large bowl; stir in sugar, nuts and carrot. Stir in combined oil, sour cream and eggs. Bake as directed.

Butter cream

Basic butter cream is also called vienna cream; the flavour can be varied by adding any extract or essence you like.

125g (4 ounces) unsalted butter, softened
1½ cups (240g) icing (confectioners') sugar
2 tablespoons milk

Beat butter in small bowl with electric mixer until as white as possible. Gradually beat in half the sifted icing sugar, milk, then remaining icing sugar.

Chocolate variation

Sift ⅓ cup (35g) cocoa powder in with the first batch of icing sugar.

Glacé icing

2¼ cups (360g) icing (confectioners') sugar
¼ cup (60ml) water, approximately
food colouring

Sift icing sugar into medium heatproof bowl, stir in enough water to give a firm paste. Colour as desired. Stir the paste over medium saucepan of hot water (the water should not touch the bottom of the bowl) until icing is spreadable; do not overheat. The bottom of the bowl should feel warm (not hot) to the touch. Use immediately.

Fluffy mock cream frosting

2 tablespoons milk
⅓ cup (80ml) water
1 cup (220g) caster (superfine) sugar
1 teaspoon gelatine
2 tablespoons water, extra
250g (8 ounces) unsalted butter, softened
1 teaspoon vanilla extract

Combine milk, the water and sugar in small saucepan; stir syrup over low heat, without boiling, until sugar is dissolved. Sprinkle gelatine over the extra water in a cup, add to pan; stir syrup until gelatine is dissolved. Cool to room temperature. Beat butter and extract in small bowl with electric mixer until it is as white as possible. While motor is operating, gradually pour in cold syrup, in a thin steady stream; beat until light and fluffy. Mixture will thicken more on standing.

Fluffy frosting

1 cup (220g) caster (superfine) sugar
⅓ cup (80ml) water
2 egg whites

Combine sugar and the water in small saucepan; stir with a wooden spoon over high heat, without boiling, until sugar dissolves. Boil, uncovered, without stirring, about 3 to 5 minutes or until syrup is slightly thick. If a candy thermometer is available, the syrup will be ready when it reaches 114°C (240°F). When the syrup is thick, remove the pan from the heat, allow the bubbles to subside then test the syrup by dropping 1 teaspoon into a cup of cold water. The syrup should form a ball of soft sticky toffee. The syrup should not change in colour; if it does, it has been cooked for too long and you will have to discard it and start again. While the syrup is boiling, and after about four minutes, beat the egg whites in a small bowl with an electric mixer until stiff; keep beating (or the whites will deflate) until syrup reaches the correct temperature. When syrup is ready, allow bubbles to subside then pour a very thin stream onto the egg whites with mixer operating on medium speed. If the syrup is added too quickly to the egg whites the frosting will not thicken. Continue beating and adding syrup until all syrup is used. Continue to beat until frosting stands in stiff peaks (frosting should be barely warm). For best results, frosting should be applied to a cake on the day it is to be served. While you can frost the cake the day before, the frosting will become crisp and lose its glossy appearance, much like a meringue.

Royal icing

1½ cups (240g) pure icing (confectioners') sugar
1 egg white
½ teaspoon lemon juice

Sift icing sugar through very fine sieve. Lightly beat egg white in a small bowl with an electric mixer; add icing sugar, a tablespoon at a time. When icing reaches firm peaks, use a wooden spoon to beat in the juice. Royal icing must be kept covered, either with a well wrung out wet cloth then plastic wrap, or with the plastic wrap pressed onto the surface of the icing. Royal icing develops a crust when it's left open to the air – this usually makes the icing unusable, particularly for piping.

Ready-made white icing

This is available from cake-decorating suppliers and some health-food shops, delicatessens and supermarkets. There are several brands available. This is very easy to use. Break off as much icing as you need; re-wrap remaining icing to exclude the air, or a crust will develop, which will spoil the smooth texture of the icing.

Knead the piece of icing on a surface lightly dusted with sifted icing sugar. If colouring the icing, start working tiny amounts of the colouring through the icing. The icing should be smooth and free from stickiness. Only work with small amounts of icing at the one time as the air will dry it out. Cover any rolled-out icing with plastic wrap.

baking information

Packet or home made cakes

Unbaked cake mixtures (both packet and home made) will tolerate standing at a cool room temperature for at least an hour.

We have used cakes made from packet mixes throughout this book for consistency of size and baking times. We used 470g (15-ounce) packets, however, there are other sizes available and they will all work with our recipes. If you want to make your own cakes, choose any of the recipes on page 106; they will all bake at similar temperatures, times, and in the same pan sizes as the packet mix cakes suggested in each recipe. One quantity of any of the cake recipes is equivalent to one 470g (15-ounce) packaged cake mix.

Beating packet mixes

It's important to beat the packet mixes properly using an electric mixer – not a food processor or blender. We found a stand-alone mixer gave us the best results, simply because it's easier to let the machine do the work rather than holding a hand-held mixer (there is a tendency to under-beat the mixture using one of these). Also, it's important to beat the packet mixes enough to develop the volume of the mixture. The ingredients should be at room temperature for best results. Start the mixer at a low speed to incorporate the ingredients, then gradually increase the speed to medium. As a rule, one packet of cake mix fits into a small bowl, two or three packets into a medium bowl, and four packets into a large bowl. The beaters should always be well down in the mixture to create volume.

Measuring cake quantities

To achieve the same results as we did for the cakes in this book, it's important to measure the mixture accurately into the correct-sized cake pans. Often there is some cake mixture left over, just use it to make more cakes for the party. Some of the cakes in this book require half-packets of cake mixture to be used, weigh or measure the contents to make sure they're halved accurately. Make sure you halve the ingredients indicated on the packet to get the balance of the mixture correct.

Baking

Fan-forced ovens should bake everything that is being cooked in the oven evenly, however, some domestic ovens have hot spots. If you need to bake cakes on two oven racks, it will be necessary to change the positions of the cakes about halfway through the baking time. It's fine to cook more than one cake on the same oven rack, but the cake pans shouldn't touch each other or the sides of the oven or the closed oven door. It's usually a good idea to change the positions of the cake pans on the same rack, too. Remember that cakes rise, allow for this when positioning the racks before the oven is preheated. As a guide, cakes should be baked in the centre of the oven, more towards the lower half of the oven. If the oven is loaded with cakes of varying sizes, they might take a little longer to bake than our recipes indicate.

Food colourings

Use good quality colourings for the best results; they will "hold" the colour in the icing. Some of the inexpensive liquid colourings will fade or darken the icing on standing. Icings or frostings based on butter are the most difficult to colour as butter is yellow, so any colour will be affected by the base colour. This is why it's important to beat the butter until it's as white as possible. We found unsalted butter to work (and taste) the best. Fluffy frosting and royal icing are the easiest to colour, because they're white to begin with. If possible (it's not with fluffy frosting), conduct a little test to ensure your icing will remain a desirable colour. Tint a small portion of the icing to the shade you want, keep it airtight, and let it stand for a few hours before colouring the whole batch.

Cake pans

There's a vast array of cake pans available from chain stores, supermarkets, cookware, homeware and hardware shops, also from shops that specialise in cake decorating supplies. Price is a guide to quality when it comes to cake pans, if you buy wisely and look after the pans, they should last a lifetime. Cake pans are made from many different materials. Uncoated aluminium pans, which are our favourite, are becoming increasingly difficult to get. There are metal pans with non-stick coating, which still need greasing, scratch easily and tend to make baked goods develop a heavy crust. Decrease the oven temperature to compensate for this. Heavy, good-quality tin pans bake cakes well, but usually work better if the goods are baked at a slightly lower temperature than normal. Inexpensive cake pans made from thin flimsy tin are not a good investment as they tend to twist and buckle, often after the first time they're used. Silicone pans are also available, cakes baked in these develop a light crust, which is sometimes a good thing. Muffins and cupcakes work particularly well in these pans.

Covering a square cake board Cut the covering paper about 5cm (2 inches) larger than the board, place the board, top-side down on the back of the paper. Use tape or glue to stick the paper to the board. If the paper is thick, cut the corners out of the paper as if covering a book.

Covering a round cake board Cut the covering paper about 5cm (2 inches) larger than the board, place the board, top-side down on the back of the paper. Snip the paper border, on an angle, all the way around. Fold each snipped piece of paper over onto the board; tape or glue the paper onto the board.

Greasing cake pans Melted butter applied evenly with a pastry brush is the best method of greasing a cake pan, particularly cake pans which are patterned, or are an unusual shape.

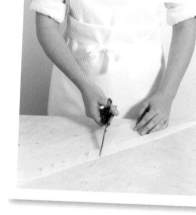

Flouring a greased cake pan We have indicated when to grease and flour cake pans. Refrigerate the greased pan for a few minutes to set the butter. Sprinkle the buttered area with flour, turn and tap the pan until the pan is floured evenly, then tap the pan over the sink or bin, to get rid of the excess flour.

Lining for a round cake pan Cut a strip of baking paper, long enough to encircle the inside of the pan and overlap slightly, plus about an extra 7cm (2¾ inches) to allow for the fold-over at the base of the pan and for the paper to extend above the side of the pan. Fold about 2cm (¾ inch) of the paper over, then snip the paper, on an angle, up to the fold.

Lightly grease the inside of the pan, to hold the lining paper in place, position the snipped paper around the side of the pan. Using the base of the pan as a guide, trace around the base of the pan. Cut out the round of paper, cutting slightly inside the marked circle. Position the paper in the pan.

Lining rectangular or square cake pans Cut strips of baking paper long enough to cover base and sides of the lightly-greased cake pan, sometimes only one strip of paper is necessary. Always extend the paper over the sides of the pan by about 5cm (2 inches).

Levelling cakes Most cakes need to have their tops cut off to make the cakes sit flat on a cake board or plate. Use a large sharp serrated knife to do this.

Preparing cakes for decorating Most of the cakes in this book are turned top-side down for decorating. There are just a few decorated top-side up, for a domed effect. Recipes will indicate when to position the cake on a cake board or plate.

Using patterns Trace the pattern from the pattern sheet provided onto paper, cut out the shape. Secure the pattern to the cake – usually the bottom of the cake – with toothpicks to hold the pattern firmly in place.

Cutting out the cake Use a small sharp serrated knife to cut carefully around the pattern. Hold the knife upright for the best results.

Brushing the cake with jam Use warmed, sieved jam – we like apricot, but use whatever jam you like – to brush over the surface of the cake, when recipes indicate this is necessary. Be particular about brushing the jam evenly and thoroughly over any cut surfaces on the cake. If the cake is fresh and crumbly, freeze it for an hour or so to make the job easier.

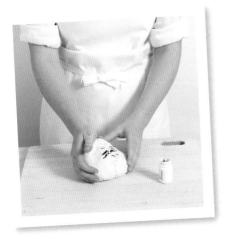

Colouring ready-made icing Use good quality food colourings for best results. Always start with a tiny dab of the colouring, work it through the icing with your fingers; determine the depth and strength of the colouring before adding any more.

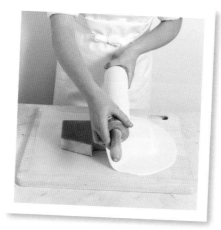

Rolling out ready-made icing Use a rolling pin to roll the icing to the correct size and thickness. Icing can be rolled on a surface dusted lightly with sifted icing sugar, or between sheets of baking paper. Use the rolling pin to lift the icing over the cake.

Smoothing ready-made icing Using icing-sugared hands, gently mould and smooth the icing around the shape of the cake. Make sure the icing feels like it is clinging to the jam on the cake.

Trimming ready-made icing Use a small sharp pointed knife to carefully trim away the excess icing from around the edge of the cake. Scraps of icing will keep well for months, if they're wrapped tightly in plastic wrap, to exclude the air.

Making fluffy mock cream Beat the softened butter in a small bowl – so that the beaters are well down into the butter – until the butter is as white as possible.

Adding syrup to fluffy mock cream Gradually add the room-temperature syrup, in a thin steady stream, to the butter while the motor is operating.

Cutting shapes from ready-made icing Use a rolling pin to roll the icing to the correct thickness, on a surface dusted with sifted icing sugar or between sheets of baking paper. Use sharp cutters to cut out shapes. Dry shapes on baking paper until firm, or apply directly to the icing on the cake while still soft.

Colouring butter cream Use a skewer to dab a tiny amount of colouring onto the butter cream, mix the colouring through the butter cream thoroughly before adding any more.

Preparing the cake for decorating If the cake is very fresh, freeze it for a few hours, or refrigerate it overnight. Using a metal spatula, apply a very thin layer of butter cream evenly over the cold cake, don't worry if crumbs become mixed with this layer of butter cream. If necessary, refrigerate or freeze the cake to set the butter cream "undercoat".

Applying the final coat of butter cream Spread the final layer of butter cream evenly over the "undercoat". If the cake feels firm, by-pass the undercoat and simply apply the final layer of butter cream to the cake.

Making fluffy frosting Beat the egg whites until stiff towards the end of the syrup's cooking time, keep beating the egg whites while the syrup reaches the correct temperature. Gradually add the hot syrup to the beating egg whites in a thin steady stream. Beat the frosting until firm peaks form.

Colouring fluffy frosting This frosting should be coloured by beating the colouring into the frosting just before the frosting is to be used. This frosting does not stand well, it should be made and used quite quickly, as it sets on standing.

Making a paper piping bag Cut a square from a sheet of baking paper, fold it in half diagonally, cut it in half along the fold to make two triangles.

Shaping the paper piping bag Hold the apex of the triangle towards you, wrap one point of the triangle around to form a cone shape, then wriggle the three points of the triangle until they line up perfectly.

Securing the paper piping bag Staple the piping bag so that the staple holds the three points of the triangle in place. Fill the bag with icing, snip a tiny piece from the point of the bag, pipe a little icing to judge if the hole is large enough, if not, snip more paper from the point of the bag.

Colouring coconut Use disposable gloves to stop the colouring staining your skin. Place the coconut into a bowl and rub drops of colouring through the coconut until it's evenly coloured. This method can be used to colour sugar too.

Colouring sugar Place the sugar into a strong resealable plastic bag with a little colouring. Massage the colouring through the sugar until it's evenly coloured. This method can also be used for colouring coconut.

Using licorice Use sharp scissors for cutting and trimming licorice into various shapes and sizes.

Making glacé icing Stir the icing over hot water until it's smooth and pourable. The icing must only ever be warm, not hot. Pour the warmed icing over the cake as quickly as possible, preferably without trying to spread it out with a spatula. The icing can be trimmed after it has set.

Melting chocolate Melt chocolate over hot water, it's important that the water in the pan doesn't touch the bottom of the bowl, so that the chocolate doesn't overheat and spoil.

Piping chocolate discs Use either small piping bags fitted with a plain piping tube, or a paper piping bag. Half-fill the bag with melted chocolate, pipe discs of chocolate onto baking paper-lined flat tray, tap the tray on the batch to make the chocolate spread slightly, leave the discs to set at room temperature.

Backing ribbon Sometimes ribbon needs to be backed, so that it doesn't become stained by the icing it's in contact with. Use a strip of adhesive tape the same width as the ribbon, and apply to the back of the ribbon. You might need help to keep the ribbon straight while doing this.

Positioning skewers for tiered cakes Consider the size of the base of the top cake, insert the skewers in the bottom cake, right through to the cake board, so that the top cake can be supported by them. Trim the skewers so that they are level with the top of the bottom cake. Position the skewers.

Carefully sit the top tier on the skewers. There will be a small gap between the two cakes, but this can be easily covered with icing or decorations. Remove the top tier, using a metal spatula, before cutting the cakes.

glossary

almonds

blanched brown skins removed.

flaked paper-thin slices.

ground also called almond meal; nuts are powdered to a coarse flour texture for use in baking or as a thickening agent.

baking paper also called parchment, silicon paper or non-stick baking paper; not to be confused with greaseproof or waxed paper. Used to line cake pans; also to make piping bags.

baking powder a raising agent consisting mainly of two parts cream of tartar to one part bicarbonate of (baking) soda.

bicarbonate of soda also called baking soda; a mild alkali used as a leavening agent in baking.

butter we use salted butter unless stated otherwise. Unsalted or "sweet" butter has no added salt.

buttermilk originally the term given to the slightly sour liquid left after butter was churned from cream, today it is made similarly to yogurt. Sold alongside milk products in supermarkets. Despite the implication of its name, it is low in fat.

cereal

Coco Pops chocolate-flavoured puffed rice.

Froot Loops fruit-flavoured puffed rice.

puffed rice gluten-free cereal made from whole brown rice grains.

Rice Bubbles puffed rice product made with malt extract; contains gluten.

chocolate

Choc Bits also called chocolate chips or chocolate morsels; available in milk, white and dark chocolate. Made of cocoa liquor, cocoa butter, sugar and an emulsifier; hold their shape in baking and are ideal for decorating.

dark cooking also called compound chocolate; good for cooking as it doesn't require tempering and sets at room temperature. Made with vegetable fat instead of cocoa butter so it lacks the rich, buttery flavour of eating chocolate. Cocoa butter is the most expensive component in chocolate, so the substitution of a vegetable fat means that compound chocolate is much cheaper to produce.

dark eating also called semi-sweet or luxury chocolate; made of a high percentage of cocoa liquor and cocoa butter, and little added sugar. Unless stated otherwise, we use dark eating chocolate in this book as it's ideal for use in desserts and cakes.

milk eating most popular eating chocolate, mild and very sweet; similar in make-up to dark, with the difference being the addition of milk solids.

melts small discs of compound milk, white or dark chocolate ideal for melting and moulding.

white eating contains no cocoa solids but derives its sweet flavour from cocoa butter. Very sensitive to heat.

chocolate hazelnut spread we use Nutella; made of cocoa powder, hazelnuts, sugar and milk.

cinnamon available in the piece (sticks or quills) and ground into powder; one of the world's most common spices.

cocoa powder also called unsweetened cocoa; cocoa beans (cacao seeds) that have been fermented, roasted, shelled, ground into powder then cleared of most of the fat content.

coconut

cream obtained commercially from the first pressing of the coconut flesh alone, without the addition of water. Available in cans and cartons at most supermarkets.

desiccated concentrated, dried, unsweetened and finely shredded coconut flesh.

essence synthetically made from flavouring, oil and alcohol.

flaked dried flaked coconut flesh.

shredded unsweetened thin strips of dried coconut flesh.

confectionery

allsorts layered sweets consisting of licorice and fondant.

bullets small lengths of licorice coated in chocolate candy.

licorice an aniseed-flavoured confection which comes in straps, tubes and twisted ropes.

Mallow Bakes coloured marshmallow pellets; made from sugar, glucose, cornflour and gelatine.

marshmallows pink and white; made from sugar, glucose, gelatine and cornflour.

Smarties small multi-coloured rounds made from chocolate, sugar and flour.

spearmint leaves soft sugar-coated, leaf-shaped sweets flavoured with spearmint.

corn syrup a sweet syrup made by heating cornstarch with water under pressure. It comes in light and dark types and is used in baking and in confectionery.

cornflour also known as cornstarch. Available made from corn or wheat (wheaten cornflour, gluten-free, gives a lighter texture in cakes); used as a thickening agent.

cream

pouring also called pure cream. It has no additives, and contains a minimum fat content of 35 per cent.

thickened a whipping cream that contains a thickener. Has a minimum fat content of 35 per cent.

cream of tartar the acid ingredient in baking powder; added to confectionery mixtures to help prevent sugar from crystallising. Keeps frostings creamy.

custard powder instant mixture used to make pouring custard; similar to North American instant pudding mixes.

eggs we use large chicken eggs (60g) in our recipes unless stated otherwise. If a recipe calls for raw or barely cooked eggs, exercise caution if there is a salmonella problem in your area.

flour

besan also called chickpea flour or gram; made from ground chickpeas so is gluten-free and high in protein.

plain also called all-purpose; unbleached wheat flour is the best for baking.

rice very fine, almost powdery, gluten-free flour; made from ground white rice.

self-raising all-purpose plain or wholemeal flour with baking powder and salt added; make at home in the proportion of 1 cup flour to 2 teaspoons baking powder.

food colouring vegetable-based substance available in liquid, paste or gel form.

gelatine a thickening agent. Available in sheet form (leaf gelatine) or as a powder – 3 teaspoons powdered gelatine (8g or one sachet) is roughly equivalent to four gelatine leaves.

ginger

fresh also called green or root ginger; the thick gnarled root of a tropical plant.

glacé fresh ginger root preserved in sugar syrup; crystallised ginger can be substituted if rinsed with warm water and dried before using.

ground also known as powdered ginger; used as a flavouring in cakes, pies and puddings but cannot be substituted for fresh ginger.

honey honey sold in a squeezable container is not suitable for the recipes in this book.

ice-cream use good-quality ice-cream; ice-cream varieties differ from manufacturer to manufacturer depending on the quantities of air and fat incorporated into the mixture.

jam also called conserve or preserve.

lollies also called sweets or candy.

milk we use full-cream homogenised milk unless stated otherwise.

Milo chocolate malted sweetened milk drink base.

mixed peel candied citrus peel.

mixed spice a classic mixture generally containing caraway, allspice, coriander, cumin, nutmeg and ginger, although cinnamon and other spices can be added. It is used with fruit and in cakes.

nutmeg a strong and very pungent spice ground from the dried nut of an evergreen tree native to Indonesia. Usually found ground but the flavour is more intense from a whole nut, available from spice shops, so it's best to grate your own. Found in mixed spice mixtures.

oil

cooking spray we use a cholesterol-free spray made from canola oil.

vegetable oils sourced from plant rather than animal fats.

popcorn a variety of corn that is sold as kernels for popping corn, or can be bought ready-popped.

poppy seeds small, dried, bluish-grey seeds of the poppy plant, with a crunchy texture and a nutty flavour. Can be purchased whole or ground in most supermarkets.

raisins dried sweet grapes (traditionally muscatel grapes).

ready-made white icing also called soft icing, ready-to-roll and prepared fondant. Available from the baking section in most supermarkets.

roasting/toasting nuts and dried coconut can be roasted in the oven to restore their fresh flavour and release their aromatic essential oils. Spread them evenly onto an oven tray then roast in a moderate oven for about 5 minutes. Desiccated coconut, pine nuts and sesame seeds roast more evenly if stirred over low heat in a heavy-based frying pan; their natural oils will help turn them golden brown.

sour cream thick, commercially-cultured sour cream with a minimum fat content of 35 per cent.

star anise a dried star-shaped pod whose seeds have an astringent aniseed flavour.

sugar we use coarse, granulated table sugar, also called crystal sugar, unless stated otherwise.

brown a very soft, fine granulated sugar retaining molasses for its characteristic colour and flavour.

caster also known as superfine or finely granulated table sugar. The fine crystals dissolve easily making it perfect for cakes, meringues and desserts.

demerara small-grained golden-coloured crystal sugar.

icing also called confectioners' sugar or powdered sugar; pulverised granulated sugar crushed together with a small amount (about 3 per cent) of cornflour.

pure icing also called confectioners' or powdered sugar; does not contain cornflour.

raw natural brown granulated sugar.

vanilla granulated or caster sugar flavoured with a vanilla bean; can be stored indefinitely.

sultanas also called golden raisins; dried seedless white grapes.

tempering the process by which chocolate is melted at a specific temperature that enables it to set with a glossy finish.

vanilla

bean dried, long, thin pod from a tropical golden orchid grown in central and South America and Tahiti; the minuscule black seeds inside the bean are used to impart a luscious vanilla flavour in baking and desserts.

essence obtained from vanilla beans infused in alcohol and water.

extract obtained from vanilla beans infused in water; a non-alcoholic version of essence.

yogurt we use plain full-cream yogurt in our recipes unless stated otherwise.

conversion chart

measures

One Australian metric measuring cup holds approximately 250ml; one Australian metric tablespoon holds 20ml; one Australian metric teaspoon holds 5ml.

The difference between one country's measuring cups and another's is within a two- or three-teaspoon variance, and will not affect your cooking results. North America, New Zealand and the United Kingdom use a 15ml tablespoon.

All cup and spoon measurements are level. The most accurate way of measuring dry ingredients is to weigh them. When measuring liquids, use a clear glass or plastic jug with metric markings.

We use large eggs with an average weight of 60g.

dry measures

METRIC	IMPERIAL
15g	½oz
30g	1oz
60g	2oz
90g	3oz
125g	4oz (¼lb)
155g	5oz
185g	6oz
220g	7oz
250g	8oz (½lb)
280g	9oz
315g	10oz
345g	11oz
375g	12oz (¾lb)
410g	13oz
440g	14oz
470g	15oz
500g	16oz (1lb)
750g	24oz (1½lb)
1kg	32oz (2lb)

liquid measures

METRIC	IMPERIAL
30ml	1 fluid oz
60ml	2 fluid oz
100ml	3 fluid oz
125ml	4 fluid oz
150ml	5 fluid oz (¼ pint)
190ml	6 fluid oz
250ml	8 fluid oz
300ml	10 fluid oz (½ pint)
500ml	16 fluid oz
600ml	20 fluid oz (1 pint)
1000ml (1 litre)	1¾ pints

length measures

METRIC	IMPERIAL
3mm	⅛in
6mm	¼in
1cm	½in
2cm	¾in
2.5cm	1in
5cm	2in
6cm	2½in
8cm	3in
10cm	4in
13cm	5¼in
15cm	6in
18cm	7¼in
20cm	8in
23cm	9¼in
25cm	10in
28cm	11¼in
30cm	12in (1ft)

oven temperatures

These oven temperatures in this book are for conventional ovens; if you have a fan-forced oven, decrease the temperature by 10-20 degrees.

	°C (CELSIUS)	°F (FAHRENHEIT)
Very slow	120	250
Slow	150	300
Moderately slow	160	325
Moderate	180	350
Moderately hot	200	400
Hot	220	425
Very hot	240	475

index

First published in 2011 by ACP Magazines Ltd,
a division of Nine Entertainment Co.
54 Park St, Sydney
GPO Box 4088, Sydney, NSW 2001.
phone (02) 9282 8618; fax (02) 9126 3702
acpbooks@acpmagazines.com.au; www.acpbooks.com.au

ACP BOOKS
General Manager - Christine Whiston
Editor-in-Chief - Susan Tomnay
Creative Director - Hieu Chi Nguyen
Art Director - Hannah Blackmore
Food Director - Pamela Clark

Published and Distributed in the United Kingdom by Octopus Publishing Group
Endeavour House
189 Shaftesbury Avenue
London WC2H 8JY
United Kingdom
phone (+44)(0)207 632 5400; fax (+44)(0)207 632 5405
info@octopus-publishing.co.uk;
www.octopusbooks.co.uk

Printed by Toppan Printing Co., China

International foreign language rights - Brian Cearnes, ACP Books bcearnes@acpmagazines.com.au

A catalogue record for this book is available from the British Library.
ISBN 978-1-74245-0544
© ACP Magazines Ltd 2011
ABN 18 053 273 546